REDISCOVERING GOD IN AMERICA

Reflections on the Role of Faith in Our Nation's History and Future

NEWT GINGRICH

Featuring the Photography of
CALLISTA GINGRICH

THOMAS NELSON
Since 1798

NASHVILLE   DALLAS   MEXICO CITY   RIO DE JANEIRO   BEIJING

Published in Nashville, Tennessee, by Thomas Nelson. Thomas Nelson is a registered trademark of Thomas Nelson, Inc.

Photo on page 81 from the Corbis Collection © CORBIS
Photo on page 4 from iStockphoto

Thomas Nelson, Inc., titles may be purchased in bulk for educational, business, fund-raising, or sales promotional use. For information, please e-mail SpecialMarkets@ThomasNelson.com.

Scripture quotations used in this book are from *The King James Version.*

Cover Design: Kristen Vasgaard

Interior Design: Walter Petrie

ISBN: 978-1-59555-313-3 (revised edition)

Library of Congress Cataloging-in-Publication Data

Gingrich, Newt.
     Rediscovering God in America / Newt Gingrich.
          p. cm.
     Summary: "Significant monuments, memorials, and artifacts found in our Nation's capital are Creator-endowed as seen through a walk through tour of Washington DC"—Provided by publisher.
     ISBN: 978-1-59145-482-3 (hardcover)
     1. Washington (D.C.)—Religion. 2. Washington (D.C.)—Buildings, structures, etc. 3. Washington (D.C.)—Description and travel. I. Title.
BL2527.W18G56 2006
200.9753—dc22   2006023450

Printed in the United States of America

09 10 11 12 13 WRZ 5 4 3 2 1

This book is dedicated to my grandmother Ethel Daugherty, my parents, Kit and Bob Gingrich, my Aunt Loma and Uncle Cal Troutman, and to Callista's parents, Alphonse and Bernita Bisek, because they taught us that God is central to our lives and to the meaning of being an American.

ACKNOWLEDGMENTS

This book is the result of great effort and determination by a number of people. As ideas were developed, we began to realize how much there is to learn about the historical leaders of our country and their devotion to God.

An earlier version of this work was published by Integrity House Publishing in 2006. The genesis of this project, however, began in 2005 as an appendix to *Winning the Future: A 21st Century Contract with America*, published by Regnery Publishing, Inc. Thanks to Jeff Carneal, president of Eagle Publishing, Marji Ross, president of Regnery Publishing, and everyone on the Regnery team for giving this work its start.

Our gratitude goes to Kathy Lubbers who, through the Lubbers Agency, managed this project, and to her husband, Paul Lubbers, who has been consistently supportive.

Invaluable writing, editing, and research assistance was provided by Jessica Gavora, Rick Tyler, Vince Haley, Joe DeSantis, Peter Oppenheim, Albert S. Hanser, Daniel P. Johnson, Kevin Goll, Sylvia Garcia, and Ross Worthington. Photographic consultation was provided by David Luria, Matthew Fry, and Robbie Gross.

Special thanks to my wife, Callista, whose photography is featured throughout this edition of *Rediscovering God in America*. It has been a real joy to work together on this project, as well as on our documentary film and audio book, based on this text.

Finally, we want to acknowledge our grandchildren, Maggie and Robert, and their parents Jackie and Jimmy Cushman. Our grandchildren have been the motivation and inspiration to help preserve the idea that is central to America's greatness: that we are all endowed by our Creator with unalienable rights to life, liberty, and the pursuit of happiness.

May we all live in an America that understands the role of God in our history, and respects His role in our national life.

WASHINGTON, DC 2009

CONTENTS

Introduction

THE CREATOR AND
THE AMERICAN PUBLIC SQUARE

There is no attack on American culture more destructive and more historically dishonest than the secular Left's relentless effort to drive God out of America's public square. The 2002 decision by the Ninth Circuit Court of Appeals that the phrase "under God" is unconstitutional represents a fundamental assault on our American identity. A court that would unilaterally modify the Pledge of Allegiance as adopted by the Congress in 1954, signed by President Eisenhower, and supported by 91 percent of the American people is a court that is clearly out of step with an America that understands that our unalienable rights come from God.

This book—a walking tour of our nation's capital—is a rebuttal to those who seek to write God out of American history. Step by step, you will see the concrete case for defending the place that America has always acknowledged for the Creator in our public life.

In the Pledge of Allegiance case, while the Supreme Court overruled the Ninth Circuit on procedural grounds, it did not affirm that saying "under God" was constitutional. Only three of the justices took that position. Five of the justices hid behind procedural excuses, ruling that the plaintiff did not have legal standing to file the suit. The ninth justice, Antonin Scalia, had recused himself because he had made a public speech supporting the Pledge.

But if the plaintiff did have legal standing, the Supreme Court might have had—amazingly—a five to four majority in 2004 for declaring "under God" unconstitutional. Justice Sandra Day O'Connor only defended the phrase "under God" in the Pledge by arguing that it was meaningless:

> Even if taken literally, the phrase is merely descriptive; it purports only to identify the United States as a Nation subject to divine authority. That cannot be seen as a serious invocation of God or as an expression of individual submission to divine authority. . . . Any religious freight the words may have been meant to carry has long since been lost.

The Pledge, she deemed, merely invoked "civic deism." Yet, if pledging allegiance to one nation *under God* does not mean we believe America is a nation *under God* (and by extension, ourselves as citizens as well), what could it possibly mean?

When a handful of judges can ignore history and decide they can overrule the culture of 91 percent of America, how can the judiciary, including the Supreme Court, maintain its moral authority? It can't. The Court itself begins each day with the proclamation, "God save the United States and this honorable Court." This phrase has been used for almost two hundred years. It was not adopted as a ceremonial phrase of no meaning; it was adopted because justices in the 1820s actually wanted to call on God to save the United States and the Court.

Similarly, the Pledge of Allegiance does not contain a "ceremonial" reference to God. The term "under God" was inserted deliberately by Congress to draw the distinction between atheistic tyranny (the Soviet Union) and a free society whose freedoms were based on the God-given rights of each person. As Supreme Court Justice William O. Douglas wrote in *Zorach vs. Clauson* just two years before the Congress added the words "under God" to the Pledge: "We are a religious people and our institutions presuppose a Supreme Being."

In the last fifty years, the Court has moved from recognizing the central importance of religious supports to America's republican institutions to tolerating traditional expressions of religious belief only on the basis of their presumed insincerity.

For most Americans, the blessings of God are the basis of our liberty, prosperity, and survival as a unique country.

For most Americans, prayer is real, and we subordinate ourselves to a God on whom we call for wisdom, guidance, and salvation.

For most Americans, the prospect of a ruthlessly secular society that would forbid public reference to God and systematically remove all religious symbols from the public square is horrifying.

Yet, the voice of the overwhelming majority of Americans is rejected by a media-academic-legal elite that finds religious expression frightening and threatening, or old-fashioned and unsophisticated. The results of their opposition are everywhere.

Our schools have been steadily driving the mention of God out of American history (look at your children's textbooks or at the curriculum guide for your local school).

Our courts have been literally outlawing references to God, religious symbols, and stated public appeals to God.

For two generations we have passively accepted the judiciary's assault on the values of the overwhelming majority of Americans. It is time to insist on judges who understand that throughout our history—and continuing to this day—Americans believe that their fundamental rights come from God and are therefore unalienable.

The secular Left has been inventing law and grotesquely distorting the Constitution to achieve a goal that the Founding Fathers would consider a fundamental threat to liberty.

A steadfast commitment to religious freedom is the very cornerstone of American liberty.

People came to America's shores to be free to practice their religious beliefs. It brought the Puritans with their desire to create a "city on a hill" that would be a beacon of religious belief and piety. The Pilgrims were another group that poured into the new colonies. Quakers in Pennsylvania were another; Catholics in Maryland yet a fourth.

One of the first things English settlers did when arriving to the new world in 1607 was to erect a cross at Cape Henry to give thanks to God for safe passage.

A religious revival, the Great Awakening in the 1730s, inspired many Americans to fight the Revolutionary War to secure their God-given freedoms. Another great religious revival in the nineteenth century inspired the abolitionists' campaign to end slavery.

It was no accident that the marching song of the Union army during the Civil War included the line "as Christ died to make men holy let us die to make men free." That phrase was later changed to "let us live to make men free." But for the men in uniform—who were literally placing their lives on the line to end slavery—they knew that the original line was the right one.

It is a testament to the genius of the Founding Fathers that they designed a practical form of government that allows religious groups the freedom to express their strong religious beliefs in the public square—a constitutional framework that avoids inter-religious conflict and discrimination, which had characterized part of the colonial period.

FIRST PRINCIPLES

For the colonists, the argument with the British government was an argument about first principles. Where did power come from? Who defined rights between king and subject? What defined loyalty?

It was in this historic context that America proclaimed in the Declaration of Independence that all people "are endowed by their Creator with certain unalienable rights, that among these are life, liberty and the pursuit of happiness." This is the proposition upon which America was based, and when Thomas Jefferson wrote these lines, he turned on its head the idea that power only came from God through the monarch and then to the people.

Jefferson's immortal words about unalienable rights coming from our Creator echoed the thinking of so many of the Founding Fathers.

Four years before the Declaration of Independence was written, John Adams wrote, "If men, through fear, fraud, or mistake, should in terms renounce and give up any essential natural right, the eternal law of reason and the great end of society, would absolutely vacate such renunciation; the right to freedom being the gift of God Almighty, it is not in the power of Man to alienate this gift, and voluntarily become a slave."

In 1775, Alexander Hamilton wrote, "The sacred rights of mankind are not to be rummaged for, among old parchments, or musty records. They are written, as with a sun beam, in the whole volume of human nature, by the hand of divinity itself; and can never be erased or obscured by mortal power."

John Dickinson, a Pennsylvania Quaker and signer of the U.S. Constitution, wrote in the same year of the Constitution's adoption that "Kings or parliaments could not give the rights essential to happiness—we claim them from a higher source—from the King of Kings and the Lord of all the Earth. They are not annexed to us by parchments or seals. They are created in us by the decrees of Providence, which establish the laws of our nature. They are born with us; and cannot be taken from us by any human power."

The Founding Fathers believed that God granted rights directly to every person. Moreover, these rights were "unalienable"—government simply had no power to take them away. Throughout the dramatic years of America's founding, religious expression was commonplace among the Founding Fathers and considered wholly compatible with the principles of the American Revolution. In 1774, the very first Continental Congress invited the Reverend Jacob Duché to begin each session with a prayer. When the war against Britain began, the Continental Congress provided for chaplains to serve with the military and be paid at the same rate as majors in the army.

During the Constitutional Convention of 1787, Benjamin Franklin (often considered one of the least religious of the Founding Fathers) proposed that the Convention begin each day with a prayer. As the oldest delegate, at age eighty-one, Franklin insisted that "the longer I live, the more convincing proofs I see of this truth—that God governs in the Affairs of Men."

Because of their belief that power had come from God to each individual, the framers began the Constitution with the words "we the people." Note that the Founding Fathers did not write "we the states." Nor did they write "we the government." Nor did they write "we the lawyers and judges" or "we the media and academic classes."

These historic facts pose an enormous problem for the secular Left. How can they explain America without addressing its religious character and heritage? If they dislike and, in many cases, fear this heritage, then how can they communicate the core nature of the American people and their experience?

The answer is that since the secular Left cannot accurately teach American history without addressing America's religious character and its religious heritage, it simply ignores the topic. If you don't teach about the Founding Fathers, you do not have to teach about our Creator. If you don't teach about Abraham Lincoln, you don't have to deal with fourteen references to God and four Bible verses in his 703-word second inaugural address. That speech is actually carved into the wall of the Lincoln Memorial in a permanent affront to every radical secularist who visits this public building. You have to wonder how soon there will be a lawsuit to scrape the references to God and the Bible off the monument so as not to offend those who hate or despise religious expression.

This is no idle threat. Dr. Michael Newdow, the radical secularist, has vowed to continue his fight in court to outlaw the words "under God," telling the *New York Times* that he intends to "ferret out all insidious uses of religion in daily life." While the Supreme Court did not find the words "under God" in the Pledge of Allegiance unconstitutional in the case brought by Newdow in 2004, Newdow instigated a similar lawsuit that was successful at the federal district court level and is now on appeal to the Ninth Circuit.

At the time of this writing, the ACLU has a lawsuit pending in the Supreme Court to remove a cross that is part of a veterans' memorial in the Mojave Desert in California. Similar lawsuits have attempted to remove a cross in another memorial honoring our veterans on Mount Soledad in San Diego, California.

Efforts by radical secularists to remove religious symbols are also being undertaken outside the courts. During his short term as president of the College of William and Mary in Virginia, Gene Nichol ordered the removal of an eighteen-inch brass cross from display on the altar in the university's historic Wren Chapel. Nichol claimed that the sight of a Christian cross in a chapel sent an unwelcoming message to some visitors. Thanks to the work of alumni and students, the cross was ultimately returned to permanent display in the chapel. Nichol's employment contract was not renewed.

Unlike Dr. Newdow, the ACLU, and Gene Nichol, the Founding Fathers, from the very birth of the United States, publicly acknowledged God as central to defining America and to securing the blessings of liberty for the new nation.

Our first president, George Washington, at his first inauguration on April 30, 1789, "put his right hand on the Bible . . . [after taking the oath] adding 'So help me God.' He then bent forward and kissed the Bible before him." In his inaugural address, Washington remarked that:

It would be peculiarly improper to omit in this first official act my fervent supplications to that Almighty Being who rules over the universe, who presides in the councils of nations, and whose providential aids can supply every human defect, that His benediction may consecrate to the liberties and happiness of the people of the United States a Government instituted by themselves for these essential purposes, and may enable every instrument employed in its administration to execute with success the functions allotted to his charge. . . . No people can be bound to acknowledge and adore the Invisible Hand which conducts the affairs of men more than those of the United States. . . . You will join with me, I trust, in thinking that there are none under the influence of which the proceedings of a new and free government can more auspiciously commence.

Then in the Thanksgiving Proclamation of October 3, 1789, Washington declared, "It is the duty of all Nations to acknowledge the Providence of Almighty God, to obey His will, to be grateful for His benefits, and humbly to implore His protection and favor." Note that Washington was not only asserting that individuals have obligations before God, but that nations do as well. At this point, the United States government was not yet a year old.

That most astute observer of early America, Alexis de Tocqueville, observed in *Democracy in America* (1835):

I do not know whether all Americans have a sincere faith in their religion, for who can read the human heart? But I am certain that they hold it to be indispensable to the maintenance of republican institutions.

This opinion is not peculiar to a class of citizens or to a party, but it belongs to the whole nation and to every rank of society.

The secular Left and the media-academic-legal elite would argue that even if de Tocqueville were right, he is irrelevant because he is writing about an earlier America. They argue that America has changed profoundly and is now a very different country. Justice O'Connor herself wrote that the phrase "under God" was adopted in 1954 when "our national religious diversity was neither as robust nor as well recognized as it is now."

Yet this is a profound misinterpretation of modern America. As Michael Novak has noted, recognizing one nation "under God" is much more important in a country as religiously diverse as America because the phrase transcends any one faith or denomination and is inclusive. Harvard professor Samuel Huntington has pointed out that "Americans tend to have a certain catholicity toward religion: All deserve respect."

More importantly, the wisdom of the Founding Fathers concerning religious liberty is just as relevant today as it was in 1787 because it reflects a fundamental insight about human nature and how men and women might best live out the political experiment in ordered liberty that they ordained in Philadelphia.

The Founders had a very straightforward belief that liberty was the purpose of a just government, but that the maintenance of this liberty among a free people would require virtue.

And if virtue was to survive, it would require "true religion," which was any religion that cultivates the virtues necessary to the protection of liberty.

Implicit within this vision of the Founding Fathers is a pluralistic sensibility. Any true religion would be therefore deserving of the respect of the government, which would include the freedom to express in public the moral principles of such a true religion.

This view that religion was an indispensable support of republican government was all encompassing among the founding generation:

> I dwell on this prospect with every satisfaction which an ardent love for my Country can inspire: since there is no truth more thoroughly established, than that there exists in the economy and course of nature, an indissoluble union between virtue and happiness, between duty and advantage, between the genuine maxims of an honest and magnanimous policy, and the solid rewards of public prosperity and felicity: Since we ought to be no less persuaded that the propitious smiles of Heaven, can never be expected on a nation that disregards the eternal rules of order and right, which Heaven itself has ordained: And since the preservation of the sacred fire of liberty, and the destiny of the Republican model of Government, are justly considered as deeply, perhaps as finally staked, on the experiment entrusted to the hands of the American people.
>
> —GEORGE WASHINGTON
> *First Inaugural Address*

> True religion affords to government its surest support.
>
> —GEORGE WASHINGTON
> *to the Synod of the*
> *Reformed Dutch Church of*
> *North America, October 1789*

Of all the dispositions and habits which lead to political prosperity, religion and morality are indispensable supports.

—GEORGE WASHINGTON
Farewell Address

We have no government armed with power capable of contending with human passions unbridled by morality and religion. Avarice, ambition, revenge, or gallantry, would break the strongest cords of our Constitution as a whale goes through a net. Our Constitution was made for a moral and religious people. It is wholly inadequate to the government of any other.

—JOHN ADAMS

Religion and good morals are the only solid foundation of public liberty and happiness.

—SAMUEL ADAMS

The politician who loves liberty sees . . . a gulph [sic] that may swallow up the liberty to which he is devoted. He knows that morality overthrown (and morality *must* fall without religion) the terrors of despotism can alone curb the impetuous passions of man, and confine him within the bonds of social duty.

—ALEXANDER HAMILTON

Without morals a republic cannot subsist any length of time; they therefore, who are decrying the Christian religion, whose morality is so sublime and pure, which denounces against the wicked, the eternal misery, and insures to the good eternal happiness, are undermining the solid foundations of morals, the best security for the duration of free governments.

—CHARLES CARROLL

Our country should be preserved from the dreadful evil of becoming enemies of the religion of the Gospel, which I have no doubt, but would be the introduction of the dissolution of government and the bonds of civil society.

—ELIAS BOUDINOT

Religion and Virtue are the only Foundations, not only of Republicanism and of all free Government, but of social felicity under all Governments and in all Combinations of human society.

—JOHN ADAMS

Reading, reflection, and time have convinced me that the interests of society require the observation of those moral precepts . . . in which all religions agree.

—THOMAS JEFFERSON

Religion is the only solid Base of morals and Morals are the only possible Support of free governments.

—GOUVERNEUR MORRIS

The only foundation for a useful education in a republic is to be laid in religion. Without this there can be no virtue, and without virtue there can be no liberty, and liberty is the object and life of all republican governments.

—BENJAMIN RUSH

For the Founders, it was abundantly clear. Religious liberty and freedom of religious expression would be indispensable supports for our democratic traditions of government and our pluralistic society.

And so they have, for over two hundred years.

It is important to recognize that the benefits of these supports accrue to people of not just one particular faith, but those of all faiths, and for all people of goodwill, whether religious, agnostic, atheist, or radical secularist. Likewise, the Founders clearly believed that the weakening of these religious supports—such as by the hostile treatment of religion in American public life—threatens to undermine the very republican institutions under which the religious and the non-religious alike find their liberties.

It is with this understanding in mind of the beliefs of America's founding generation that it becomes very clear why our national leaders have consistently invoked the protection of divine Providence in times of great national strife. It didn't happen for the first time in 1954 when the Congress added the words "under God" to the Pledge. On July 2, 1776, as the Continental Congress was meeting in Philadelphia to declare independence, George Washington was gathering his troops on Long Island to meet the British in battle. Washington wrote in the general orders to his men that day:

The time is now near at hand which must probably determine whether Americans are to be freemen or slaves. . . . The fate of unborn millions will now depend, *under God,* on the courage and conduct of this army.

The very same week we were declaring our independence from Great Britain, Washington was asserting that American independence ultimately depended on God.

Likewise, Abraham Lincoln, in his Gettysburg Address, remarked that:

> It is for us the living, rather, to be dedicated here to the unfinished work which they who fought here have thus far so nobly advanced. It is rather for us to be here dedicated to the great task remaining before us that from these honored dead we take increased devotion to the cause for which they gave the last full measure of devotion; that we here highly resolve that these dead shall not have died in vain; that this nation, *under God,* shall have a new birth of freedom; and that government of the people, by the people, for the people, shall not perish from the earth.

Like Washington before him, Lincoln understood that America's new birth of freedom would require that the nation seek the source of its liberties in the same place it had prior to the Civil War—under God.

In the ongoing effort to reject the founding generation's vision for religious liberty by removing any form of religious expression from American public life, the courts and the classroom are the two principal places at the center of this fight. These are the two arenas in which the secular Left has imposed change against the wishes of the overwhelming majority of Americans. Yet if we insist on courts that follow the facts of American history in interpreting the Constitution, we will reestablish the right of every American to publicly acknowledge our Creator as the source of our rights, our well being, and our wisdom. And if we insist on patriotic education both for our children and for new immigrants, we will preserve the "mystic chords of memory" that have made America the most exceptional nation in history.

For these reasons, this "walking tour" of our nation's capital is so timely and important. This tour is not just a tour of Washington, D.C.; it is a tour of American history, of the great men and women, events, documents, and institutions that are at the heart of our identity as a people and our freedom as Americans. As you read the pages of this book, you will discover that our nation was indeed founded "under God." The tour begins with the National Archives where you will find the original Declaration of Independence. It is in this document that you will find the immortal phrase declaring that we "are endowed by our Creator with certain unalienable rights."

This was the beginning of our independence as a free people.

Rediscovering God
in America

ENDOWED BY OUR CREATOR

The National Archives

"God governs in the affairs of men.
And if a sparrow cannot fall to
the ground without His notice,
is it probable that an empire
can rise without His aid?"

BENJAMIN FRANKLIN

Signer of the Declaration of Independence
and the Constitution

Chapter 1

THE NATIONAL ARCHIVES

National Archives

The National Archives is the repository of our nation's most important documents, and thus it is no coincidence that it is the first stop on our walking tour. Upon walking into the building, you will see an image of the Ten Commandments engraved in bronze on the floor, signifying that our legal system has its origin in the Ten Commandments that God gave to Moses on Mount Sinai. The Judeo-Christian beliefs brought by the Pilgrims and others to the New World formed the foundation of our Constitution and our system of laws today.

Ten Commandments in Bronze, National Archives

A BRIEF HISTORY
OF THE NATIONAL ARCHIVES

The National Archives and Records Administration is the federal agency tasked with maintaining and preserving America's historic documents and federal records. In addition, it officially publishes executive orders from the president and laws passed by Congress. Before the National Archives was established, each individual federal agency was required to keep its own records. This changed in 1934, when Congress voted to centralize the process by creating a federal agency to oversee all of the government's records. The National Archives also works to promote the public's access to government documents.

The Archives contains a stunning array of historical treasures, including, most famously, the Declaration of Independence, the Constitution, and the Louisiana Purchase Treaty. Other government records and correspondence in military, civilian, and diplomatic spheres are also preserved in the National Archives. The Archives preserves only two or three percent of the federal government's records each year, including only those documents decided to have some inherent historical or research value. The Archives also saves records that may be of interest to citizens, such as ship passenger lists and pension and military service records.

The design of the National Archives fell to John Russell Pope, who designed it with traditional Corinthian columns that allowed the structure to complement the other Greek- and Roman-inspired architecture in Washington, D.C., including the Treasury Department, the White House, the Capitol, and the Lincoln and Jefferson Memorials. Work began in 1931 and was completed in 1935. It has windowless and temperature-controlled rooms for document preservation and reproduction.

The sensitive and historic documents, such as the Constitution and the Declaration of Independence, are sealed in bronze encasings, which have had the air replaced by helium, providing a more protective

The Declaration of Independence and the Constitution of the United States

environment for the documents. Light is filtered out to avoid damage, and the documents are lowered into a protective vault after the building closes.

THE DECLARATION OF INDEPENDENCE

As the most consequential document of freedom in human history, the Declaration of Independence is the most important document held in the National Archives.

The Declaration of Independence was heavily influenced by the Magna Carta of 1215, a contract of rights between the British king and his barons generally regarded as the first great step toward guaranteed liberties in Britain. However, the Declaration of Independence differs from the Magna Carta in one essential way: the Founding Fathers believed that our rights as human beings come from God, not from the king or the state. Within the Declaration, the Founding Fathers declared their beliefs about the relationship between individual rights and human freedom, and boldly proclaimed these rights as self-evident truths. They affirmed that all people "are endowed by their Creator with certain unalienable rights, that among these are life, liberty and the pursuit of happiness." Thus, they rejected the notion that power came through the monarch to the people, but rather, directly from God.

The Declaration of Independence contains four references to God: as Lawmaker ("the laws of nature and nature's God"); as Creator ("endowed by their Creator with certain unalienable rights"); as Supreme Judge ("the Supreme Judge of the world for the rectitude of our intentions"); and as Protector ("the protection of Divine Providence").

The Declaration of Independence represents both the genesis and heart of American liberty. Our rights come from our Creator, not the government, sovereign, or king.

President John Quincy Adams raised the connection between Christianity and the Declaration at a speech given on Independence Day 1837 at Newburyport. He queried:

> Is it not that the Declaration of Independence first organized the social compact on the foundation of the Redeemer's mission upon earth? That it laid the cornerstone of human government upon the first precepts of Christianity?

The Declaration of Independence provides the proper context through which to understand the United States Constitution and Bill of Rights, with a renewed focus on the nature of the rights these documents were designed to protect.

THE CONSTITUTION AND BILL OF RIGHTS

Another document housed in the National Archives is the Constitution of the United States. Because of their belief that each person's unalienable rights come from God, the authors of the Constitution began the document with these three historic words: "We the people." Notice that they did not write "we the states" or "we the government." The Founders rejected the notion that such entities were sources of freedom and liberty.

The first ten amendments to the Constitution are known as the Bill of Rights. Amendment I begins: "Congress shall make no law respecting an establishment of religion, or prohibiting the free exercise thereof."

Contrary to those who want to eliminate religious expression from the public square, these important words were written to protect freedom *of* religion, not freedom *from* religion. The language clearly prohibits the establishment of an official national religion, while at the same time protecting the observance of religion in both private and public spaces. In fact, two of the principal authors of the First Amendment, Thomas Jefferson and James Madison, who were also our third and fourth presidents, respectively, both attended church services in the Capitol building, the most public of American spaces. During Jefferson's presidency, church services were also held in the Treasury building and the Supreme Court. Therefore, these Founding Fathers clearly saw no conflict in opposing the establishment of an official religion while protecting the freedom of religious expression in the public square.

The Declaration of Independence, Constitution, and Bill of Rights all show that America's Founding Fathers intended to forge a nation under God. These are only a few of the treasured documents housed in the National Archives, but together they form the foundation for the freedoms all Americans enjoy today.

THE INVISIBLE HAND OF GOD

The Washington Monument

*"It is the duty of all nations to
acknowledge the providence
of Almighty God and
to obey His will."*

GEORGE WASHINGTON
First President of the United States

Chapter 2

THE WASHINGTON MONUMENT

Washington Monument

From the base of the Washington Monument to its aluminum capstone, this memorial to our first president is filled with references
to our Creator. This is no coincidence, as George Washington was a
profoundly religious man.

Washington took the oath of office on April 30, 1789, with his hand
on the Bible. Immediately following the oath, Washington added, "So
help me God," and bent forward and kissed the Bible before him. He
then delivered America's first inaugural address, in which he made
note of America's indebtedness to our Creator, stating:

> No people can be bound to acknowledge and adore the invisible hand
> which conducts the affairs of men more than the people of the United
> States. Every step by which they have advanced to the character of an
> independent nation seems to have been distinguished by some token of
> Providential agency.

A BRIEF HISTORY OF THE
WASHINGTON MONUMENT

Although construction of the Washington Monument began in 1848,
a tribute to Washington had been planned since the city's inception. In
fact, Major Charles Pierre L'Enfant, the French landscape engineer who
laid out the city, allotted an area for an "Equestrian statue" of Washington
in his original design in 1783. The monument was also intended to serve
as a tomb for Washington, although his will explicitly dictated that his
burial was to be in Mount Vernon. Other proposals for a monument
eventually gained momentum, although construction of the monument
continued to be hampered by a dearth of funding.

The Washington National Monument Society was formed in 1833 to raise funds for the project, raising just under $30,000 by 1847. Architect Robert Mills' design was chosen, and construction began in 1848. (Mills had built a similar 200-foot obelisk monument to Washington in Baltimore years earlier.)

The monument was initially to be constructed on a north-south axis with the White House, although this plan had to be scrapped because soil tests indicated the ground was ill suited for such a large structure. (The city of Washington, D.C.—as locals will readily attest—feels like a swamp during the hottest summer months, not least because much of the city was actually built on marshland. This often proved problematic in the construction of large buildings such as the Washington Monument.) Thus, the monument was constructed on a site to the southeast of a true north-south axis with the White House, although on a perfect east-west axis with the Capitol. The ceremonial cornerstone was laid on July 4, 1848, with much fanfare, although the stone was eventually covered up during the construction, and its exact location is unknown today.

By 1854 the Washington National Monument Society was out of money, and construction came to a creaking halt, the monument standing at 156 feet. To spur construction, the Society invited states (and eventually foreign governments) to donate stones to the construction of the monument. The Vatican donated a stone, a move that so infuriated the xenophobic and anti-Catholic "Know-Nothing" party that they stole the stone and, bizarrely, seized control of the monument. Construction and fundraising limped along until it was halted altogether in 1861. Only 176 feet tall at that point, the monument had the forlorn appearance of a "hollow, oversized chimney," according to Mark

Twain. (Today, one can see precisely where the construction ended on the monument, due to the difference in the shade of stone used to complete the monument.)

In 1876, Congress appropriated $2 million toward the completion of the monument, and work progressed more or less without delay until the project's completion on December 6, 1884. The day was commemorated by a ceremony placing an aluminum capstone atop the monument. The east side of the capstone reads the Latin inscription *Laus Deo,* which means "Praise be to God."

GOD IN THE WASHINGTON MONUMENT

The cornerstone of the Washington Monument was laid in 1848. Although its exact location is unknown, many items were placed inside of it, including a Holy Bible and a gift from the Bible Society. They were placed alongside copies of the Declaration of Independence and U.S. Constitution.

As you walk inside the monument, you will see a memorial plaque from the Free Press Methodist-Episcopal Church, which was donated in 1893 by the Sabbath School Children of the Philadelphia Congregation. This is the first of many references to God, including a prayer offered by the city of Baltimore on the twelfth landing, a memorial offered by Chinese Christians on the twentieth landing, and a presentation made by Sunday school children from New York and Philadelphia on the twenty-fourth landing.

Other carved tribute blocks in the Washington Monument include: "Holiness to the Lord"; "Search the Scriptures"; "The memory of the just is blessed"; "May Heaven to this union continue its beneficence"; "In God We Trust"; and "Train up a child in the way he should go, and when he is old, he will not depart from it."

THE FAITH OF GEORGE WASHINGTON

Historians have long debated the extent of George Washington's faith. However, as historian Michael Novak has recently observed, "Washington's own step-granddaughter, 'Nelly' Custis, thought his words and actions were so plain and obvious that she could not understand how anybody failed to see that he had always lived as a serious Christian." She provided some of these important details to one of Washington's earliest biographers:

> It was his custom to retire to his library at nine or ten o'clock, where he remained an hour before he went to his chamber. He always rose before the sun, and remained in his library until called to breakfast. I never witnessed his private devotions, I never inquired about them. I should have thought it the greatest heresy to doubt his firm belief in Christianity. His life, his writings, prove that he was a Christian. He was not one of those who act or pray "that they may be seen of men." He communed with his God in secret.

Washington's own actions during his lifetime further show that he was a man strong in faith, despite the fact that he may have been less vocal in expressing his beliefs in public. For example, during the first meeting of the Continental Congress in Philadelphia in September 1774,

George Washington prayed alongside the other delegates, including Patrick Henry, John Jay, and Edmund Randolph, as they received the news that war with England had erupted in Boston. Here Anabaptists, Quakers, Congregationalists, Episcopalians, Unitarians, and Presbyterians all recited Psalm 35 together as patriots.

George Washington also proclaimed the first national day of thanksgiving in the United States. In 1795 he offered a proclamation of prayer and thanksgiving to the nation. His entire proclamation follows:

> When we review the calamities which afflict so many other nations, the present condition of the United States affords much matter of consolation and satisfaction. Our exemption hitherto from foreign war, an increasing prospect of the continuance of that exemption, the great degree of internal tranquility we have enjoyed, the recent confirmation of that tranquility by the suppression of an insurrection which so wantonly threatened it, the happy course of our public affairs in general, the unexampled prosperity of all classes of our citizens, are circumstances which peculiarly mark our situation with indications of the Divine beneficence toward us. In such a state of things it is in an especial manner our duty as a people, with devout reverence and affectionate gratitude, to acknowledge our many and great obligations to Almighty God and to implore Him to continue and confirm the blessings we experience. Deeply penetrated with this sentiment, I, George Washington, President of the United States, do recommend to all religious societies and denominations, and to all persons whomsoever, within the United States to set apart and observe Thursday, the 19th day of February next, as a day of public thanksgiving and prayer, and on that day to meet together and render their sincere and hearty thanks to the Great Ruler

of Nations for the manifold and signal mercies which distinguish our lot as a nation, particularly for the possession of constitutions of government which unite and by their union establish liberty with order; for the preservation of our peace, foreign and domestic; for the seasonable control which has been given to a spirit of disorder in the suppression of the late insurrection, and generally, for the prosperous course of our affairs, public and private; and at the same time humbly and fervently to beseech the kind Author of these blessings graciously to prolong them to us; to imprint on our hearts a deep and solemn sense of our obligations to Him for them; to teach us rightly to estimate their immense value; to preserve us from the arrogance of prosperity, and from hazarding the advantages we enjoy by delusive pursuits; to dispose us to merit the continuance of His favors by not abusing them; by our gratitude for them, and by a correspondent conduct as citizens and men; to render this country more and more a safe and propitious asylum for the unfortunate of other countries; to extend among us true and useful knowledge; to diffuse and establish habits of sobriety, order, morality, and piety, and finally, to impart all the blessings we possess, or ask for ourselves, to the whole family of mankind.

UPON THE ALTAR OF GOD

The Jefferson Memorial

"God who gave us life gave us liberty. Can the liberties of a nation be secure when we have removed a conviction that these liberties are the gift of God?"

THOMAS JEFFERSON
Third President of the United States

Chapter 3

THE JEFFERSON MEMORIAL

Jefferson Memorial

To those who have not been to the Jefferson Memorial, its inclusion in this book may seem surprising. After all, history has recorded Thomas Jefferson as a deist. He was the author of the famous letter to the Danbury Baptists in which he called for a "wall of separation between church and state." However, while it is true that Jefferson often stressed the importance of questioning all things, including the existence of

President Thomas Jefferson, Jefferson Memorial

God, his writings and governing history make it clear that he himself had a deep conviction that American liberties are a gift from God.

A BRIEF HISTORY OF THE
JEFFERSON MEMORIAL

It was not until 1934 that Franklin Delano Roosevelt persuaded Congress to pass a joint resolution to establish a memorial commission to honor America's third president, one of our greatest statesmen, political philosophers, and diplomats. After a myriad of different designs and location proposals, the Thomas Jefferson Memorial Commission decided to honor Pierre L'Enfant's original plan, which called for the placement of five different memorials aligned in a cross-like manner across the center of the city. The Jefferson Memorial would be the fifth and final point, along the scenic Tidal Basin.

However, in a stunningly undemocratic and un-Jeffersonian manner, the Commission solicited only one proposal, eventually approving architect John Russell Pope's design of a Pantheon-like structure for the memorial. Pope modeled his original design on Jefferson's own home, incorporating the Roman architecture Jefferson so admired into the memorial. Pope's death in 1937 spurred a renewed debate about the memorial's design. The uncompetitive bidding process served only to underscore the memorial's detractors, who now fought Pope's design and heralded the entire process as an affront to the very man the memorial was supposed to honor. Eventually, with FDR's support, Pope's Pantheon design—although slightly modified—was approved and construction on the memorial finally began. After its completion, the memorial was officially dedicated in 1943.

ALMIGHTY GOD HATH CREATED THE MIND FREE. ALL ATTEMPTS TO INFLUENCE IT BY TEMPORAL PUNISHMENTS OR BURTHENS···ARE A DEPARTURE FROM THE PLAN OF THE HOLY AUTHOR OF OUR RELIGION···NO MAN SHALL BE COMPELLED TO FREQUENT OR SUPPORT ANY RELIGIOUS WORSHIP OR MINISTRY OR SHALL OTHERWISE SUFFER ON ACCOUNT OF HIS RELIGIOUS OPINIONS OR BELIEF, BUT ALL MEN SHALL BE FREE TO PROFESS AND BY ARGUMENT TO MAINTAIN, THEIR OPINIONS IN MATTERS OF RELIGION. I KNOW BUT ONE CODE OF MORALITY FOR MEN WHETHER ACTING SINGLY OR COLLECTIVELY.

Text establishing religious freedom in 1777, Jefferson Memorial

RELIGIOUS REFERENCES
IN THE JEFFERSON MEMORIAL

Upon entering the Jefferson Memorial, if you look directly above you, around the chamber on the interior dome is the following quote: "I have sworn upon the altar of God, eternal hostility against every form of tyranny over the minds of man."

Of the four panels inside the dome, three contain references to God. As you look up at Panel One, you will see a famous passage from the Declaration of Independence:

We hold these truths to be self-evident: That all men are created equal, that they are endowed by their Creator with certain unalienable rights, that among these are life, liberty, and the pursuit of happiness.

Panel Two is excerpted from A Bill for Establishing Religious Freedom, 1777 (passed by the Virginia Assembly in 1786). It reads, in part:

Almighty God hath created the mind free. All attempts to influence it by temporal punishments or burthens . . . are a departure from the plan of the Holy Author of our religion . . . No man shall be compelled to frequent or support any religious worship or ministry or shall other-wise suffer on account of his religious opinions or belief, but all men shall be free to profess and by argument to maintain, their opinions in matters of religion. I know but one code of morality for men whether acting singly or collectively.

Finally, you will see that Panel Three, just to the left of the entrance, is taken from Jefferson's 1785 Notes on the State of Virginia. It reads:

> God who gave us life gave us liberty. Can the liberties of a nation be secure when we have removed a conviction that these liberties are the gift of God? Indeed I tremble for my country when I reflect that God is just, that His justice cannot sleep forever. Commerce between master and slave is despotism. Nothing is more certainly written in the book of fate than that these people are to be free.

Many of Jefferson's actions throughout his lifetime are indicative of his support for religion in American public life. For example, he allowed the use of public buildings for church services, including the U.S. Capitol Building. Jefferson also recommended that Congress provide one hundred dollars from the federal treasury every year for the furtherance of a Catholic missionary priest to the Kaskaskia Indian tribe. Also, when Thomas Jefferson wrote the first plan of education adopted by the District of Columbia, he used the Bible and Isaac Watts' hymnal as the principal texts for teaching reading to students.

Jefferson himself rebuffed those who claimed he was hostile toward religion. In an April 21, 1802, letter to Dr. Benjamin Rush, Jefferson wrote that his views "are the result of a life of inquiry and reflection, and very different from the anti-Christian system imputed to me by those who know nothing of my opinions."

If you have the time, visit the Jefferson exhibit below the rotunda. In contrast to what you see in the rotunda, you will notice that there is a relative lack of quotes, notes, or references to God and Jefferson's deep religious faith. This exhibit is less reflective of Jefferson and more indicative of increasing attempts to secularize public life at the expense of historical accuracy.

The next time a secularist friend uses the phrase "the wall of separation between church and state" to explain why no public funds should go toward supporting activities sponsored by religious bodies, simply inform them of Jefferson's writings and his actions while in office, such as sanctioning the use of the Capitol for church services. Ask them, "Given Jefferson's actions while in office, do you think he would agree with your plans to strip all religious activity from the public square when he himself did not?"

HE WHO MADE THE WORLD STILL GOVERNS IT

The Lincoln Memorial

*"I am profitably engaged in
reading the Bible. Take all
of this Book upon reason that you can,
and the balance by faith, and
you will live and die a better man."*

ABRAHAM LINCOLN
Sixteenth President of the United States

Chapter 4

THE LINCOLN MEMORIAL

Lincoln Memorial

From the Jefferson Memorial, we turn to the Lincoln Memorial, honoring Abraham Lincoln, who as president led our country through the Civil War. It is fitting that these two memorials share such proximity, because they should be viewed consecutively. As discussed earlier, Jefferson understood that our rights come from our Creator. Abraham Lincoln was guided by the same insight. He relied upon the power of divine Providence to guide the nation through the Civil War.

President Abraham Lincoln, Lincoln Memorial

A BRIEF HISTORY OF THE LINCOLN MEMORIAL

Like most other monuments in Washington, D.C., the process of agreeing on a design for and the placement of the Lincoln Memorial proved a taxing and controversial task. Although the idea of a memorial for Lincoln had been floated since the sixteenth president's assassination, a lack of financial support stalled any progress on such efforts.

President Taft supported an effort by Congressmen Shelby M. Cullom and Joseph G. Cannon—both of whom had known Lincoln in Illinois—to construct a memorial. Congress allocated two million dollars for the project, and after a rancorous debate to decide the memorial's design and placement, construction began in 1914 on the west end of the present-day National Mall, then called the "Potomac Flats."

Architect Henry Bacon's design was heavily influenced by Greek architecture, and he chose to model the memorial on a Greek temple known as the Parthenon (not to be confused with the Pantheon, which is Roman). The construction efforts were slow, as much of the area on which the memorial now sits was previously covered by a swamp, making the building of a foundation particularly time-consuming and difficult. Despite such problems, work on the memorial proceeded, and eight years after it was begun, President Warren Harding dedicated it on May 30, 1922.

Bacon chose the Greek Doric columns in part to symbolize Lincoln's fight to preserve democracy during the Civil War. It was apparently only incidental that Bacon created thirty-six columns, which he later decided would serve as a representation of the thirty-six states comprising the Union at the time of Lincoln's death. Above each column is an inscription of the state it represents. Since the memorial was completed in 1922, when there were forty-eight states, an additional listing of the states at the time is included in the exterior attic walls.

Daniel Chester French sculpted the statue of Lincoln, seeking to portray the president's most admired qualities, both his compassionate nature and his unyielding resolve in preserving the Union. Visitors to the memorial will notice that one of Lincoln's hands is clenched tightly, meant to indicate his determination and strength, while the other is open and relaxed, demonstrating the president's compassion.

Clenched fist, Lincoln Memorial

The imposing style of both the large Doric columns and the statue of Lincoln himself are meant to depict the strength of the Union, held together through the tireless efforts of Lincoln. Students of history will recall the difficulty the Union experienced during the war's early years, as initial military setbacks and heavy casualties led some to call for an end to the war. Lincoln, however, pressed on, confident in the moral justice of the Union's cause and also of the necessity of preserving the Union, as the "last, best hope on earth."

Children admire the Lincoln Memorial

LINCOLN'S RELIGIOUS REFLECTIONS DISPLAYED IN THE MONUMENT

Lincoln's reflections on God's role in American history are prominently displayed in his memorial. On the left side of the statue, inscribed into the wall, is the Gettysburg Address. The speech is only 267 words long, but it concludes with Lincoln's view of America's relationship to God: "We here highly resolve that these dead shall not have died in vain, that this nation, under God, shall have a new birth of freedom."

Lincoln's second inaugural address, considered by some to be his greatest speech, is inscribed into the wall on the right side of the statue. Although a mere 703 words, the address mentions God fourteen times and references the Bible four times. Here, Lincoln reflects that the course of the Civil War was not controlled by man, but by the Almighty, whose purposes were different from either side in the great conflict:

Each [Union and Confederate] looked for an easier triumph, and a result less fundamental and astounding. Both read the same Bible, and pray to the same God; and each invokes his aid against the other. It may seem strange that any men should dare to ask a just God's assistance in wringing their bread from the sweat of other men's faces; but let us judge not, that we be not judged. The prayers of both could not be answered—that of neither has been answered fully. The Almighty has his own purposes.

As you can see, Lincoln laments the destruction caused by the Civil War and urges his fellow Americans to "judge not, that we be not judged." Lincoln then ended his address with an appeal to charity in healing the wounds of war, concluding:

With malice toward none, with charity for all, with firmness in the right as God gives us to see the right, let us strive on to finish the work we are in, to bind up the nation's wounds, to care for him who shall have borne the battle and for his widow and his orphan, to do all which may achieve and cherish a just and lasting peace among ourselves and with all nations.

Nearly one hundred years following Lincoln's second inaugural, it was altogether fitting that the great civil rights leader Reverend Martin Luther King, Jr., delivered his famous "I have a dream" speech on the steps of the Lincoln Memorial. An inscription in the granite approach to the memorial was added in August 2003. Based on the text of Isaiah 40:4–5, it reads:

I have a dream that one day every valley shall be exalted, and every hill and mountain shall be made low, the rough places will be made plain, and the crooked places will be made straight and the glory of the Lord shall be revealed and all flesh shall see it together.

THE FAITH OF ABRAHAM LINCOLN

Abraham Lincoln relied on the power of divine Providence to guide the nation through four long years of a civil war which cost over 620,000 American lives. On October 16, 1862, Lincoln wrote:

If I had my way, this war would never have been commenced. If I had been allowed my way, this war would have been ended before this. But we find it still continues; and we must believe that He permits it for some wise purpose of His own, mysterious and unknown to us; and though with our limited understanding, we may not be able to compre-hend it, yet we cannot but believe, that He who made the world still governs it.

At a White House dinner during the war, the clergyman who gave the benediction closed with a thought: "The Lord is on the Union's side," to which Lincoln responded: "I am not at all concerned about that, for I know that the Lord is always on the side of the right. But it is my constant anxiety and prayer that I and this nation should be on the Lord's side."

In an earlier setting, Lincoln's dependence on God was vividly recounted in a story that he told General Dan Sickles, who had participated in the Battle of Gettysburg:

> Well, I will tell you how it was. In the pinch of the campaign up there [at Gettysburg] when everybody seemed panic stricken and nobody could tell what was going to happen, oppressed by the gravity of our affairs, I went to my room one day and locked the door and got down on my knees before Almighty God and prayed to Him mightily for victory at Gettysburg. I told Him that this war was His war, and our cause His cause, but we could not stand another Fredericksburg or Chancellorsville. And after that, I don't know how it was, and I cannot explain it, but soon a sweet comfort crept into my soul. The feeling came that God had taken the whole business into His own hands and that things would go right at Gettysburg and that is why I had no fears about you. [July 5, 1863]

In the November following the Battle of Gettysburg—the same month as the Gettysburg Address—Lincoln proclaimed that the last Thursday of November should henceforth be set aside as a day of thanksgiving. Many days of thanksgiving had been proclaimed by presidents before this one, but this proclamation is the one that finally made Thanksgiving the national holiday that we celebrate annually. Lincoln explained:

It has seemed to me fit and proper that they [gifts of God] should be solemnly, reverently, and gratefully acknowledged as with one heart and one voice by the whole American people. I do, therefore, invite my fellow-citizens in every part of the United States, and also those who are at sea and those who are sojourning in foreign lands, to set apart and observe the last Thursday of November next as a day of thanksgiving and praise to our beneficent Father who dwelleth in the heavens. [October 3, 1863]

A year later, upon receiving a gift of a Bible from a group of African-Americans from Baltimore, Lincoln offered these words of thanks:

In regard to this great book, I have but to say, it is the best gift God has given to men. All the good Savior gave to the world was communicated through this book. But for it we could not know right from wrong. All things most desirable for man's welfare, here and hereafter, are to be found portrayed in it. To you I return my most sincere thanks for the elegant company of the great Book of God which you present. [September 9, 1864]

When I hear radical secularists declare that the discussion of God should be stripped from the classrooms, I want to ask them, "How can our students understand Lincoln during the Civil War without understanding his faith in the principles of the Declaration of Independence, his meditations on Divine Will, and his firm resolution expressed at Gettysburg that this nation, *under God,* shall have a new birth of freedom?"

WE HONOR YOU

Vietnam Veterans Memorial

"Our young friends—yes, young friends, for in our hearts you will always be young, full of the love that is youth, love of life, love of joy, love of country—you fought for your country and for its safety and for the freedom of others with strength and courage. We love you for it. We honor you. And we have faith that, as He does all His sacred children, the Lord will bless you and keep you, the Lord will make His face to shine upon you and give you peace, now and forever more."

RONALD REAGAN
Fortieth President of the United States

Chapter 5

Vietnam Veterans Memorial

The Wall, Vietnam Veterans Memorial

The Vietnam Veterans Memorial has no obvious references to God, but it has been included in this tour for this reason: its creation has inspired hundreds of mementos left at the memorial that serve as a testament to the centrality of God in American life.

A BRIEF HISTORY OF THE
VIETNAM VETERANS MEMORIAL

The Vietnam Veterans who founded the Vietnam Veterans Memorial Fund, Inc. (VVMF) in 1979 had a tough challenge. The Vietnam War was one of the most divisive and politically unpopular wars in the nation's history. Over 58,000 Americans were killed and thousands more were missing in action or prisoners of war. It had only been four years since President Ford officially ended the United States' involvement in Vietnam and the bitterness was still palpable throughout the nation.

So how could the members of the VVMF create a memorial honoring the Americans who served in the Vietnam War without causing a firestorm of controversy? How could they create an opportunity for the nation to begin reconciliation with itself so the healing process could begin?

Their answer was to create a memorial that would honor and remember those that served in Vietnam without making a political statement about the war. For that reason, the memorial was named the Vietnam Veterans Memorial, instead of the Vietnam War Memorial.

On July 1, 1980, Congress authorized the construction of the memorial next to the reflecting pool that sits at the base of the Lincoln Memorial. In October the VVMF held a design competition that attracted over 1,400 entries. Their jury unanimously selected the design of a twenty-one-year-old student at Yale University named Maya Ying Lin. Final approval for the design was received on March 11, 1982. Fifteen days later, ground was formally broken.

The memorial initially had two parts: the Wall of Names, completed in November 1982, and the Three Servicemen Statue, created by American sculptor, Frederick Hart, added in November 1984 because of the controversy surrounding the original memorial's design of the wall only. President Ronald Reagan then accepted the completed memorial on behalf of the nation, and custodial service was turned over to the National Park Service's National Capital Region. The Vietnam Women's Memorial was added in November 1993.

A LIVING MEMORIAL

Every day, the park service collects mementos left by visitors to the Vietnam Veterans Memorial for their fallen loved ones. Thousands are collected, catalogued, and placed in storage each year by the park service. When the memorial first opened, people did not know that the mementos would be saved and collected, but they left them anyway. In the first two years, 554 objects were collected. The most recent count is over 50,000 objects.

Thus, as the Vietnam Veterans Memorial has become a living public memorial, it is only natural that Americans would leave religious symbols at the memorial. The National Park Service estimates that hundreds of Bibles, rosaries, and "personal considerations distinguished by scriptural passages" have been left by visitors and added to this collection. The most common sight at the memorial is to see friends, family, and comrades of the deceased rubbing a special gold crayon on a piece of paper against the wall to carefully and reverently take home that person's name as a precious keepsake. It is likewise common to see these friends, family members, and comrades bowing their heads in silent prayer. These mementos and expressions of faith have become part of the Vietnam Veterans Memorial experience and a powerful testament to the centrality of God and faith in the lives of so many Americans.

Three Servicemen Statue, Vietnam Veterans Memorial

Vietnam Women's Memorial ©

In October 1992, over 1,500 of these mementos were put on display at the Smithsonian Institution in Washington, D.C. Since then, the exhibit has traveled as far as London, England. The Imperial War Museum in London and the Jersey Explorer Children's Museum in East Orange, New Jersey, still display many of the objects.

THE VIETNAM WOMEN'S MEMORIAL

This memorial highlighting the service of women in Vietnam was added in November 1993. The statue depicts three women with a wounded soldier. One nurse comforts the soldier. Another looks for help from above while another kneels. Are these two nurses reaching out to God in prayer? The artist, Glenna Goodacre of Dallas, Texas, purposefully left the statue open to interpretation.

GIVE US FAITH
IN THEE

The Franklin Delano Roosevelt Memorial

"O Lord, give us faith. Give us faith in Thee;
faith in our sons; faith in each other;
faith in our united crusade.
Thy will be done, Almighty God. Amen."

FRANKLIN DELANO ROOSEVELT
Thirty-second President of the United States

Chapter 6

THE FRANKLIN DELANO ROOSEVELT MEMORIAL

As we approach the waterfalls of the Franklin Delano Roosevelt Memorial, it is good to keep in mind the heritage that this great president left us. Many consider Franklin Roosevelt to be the father of modern liberalism, so it may surprise you to know that he was a man of deep religious conviction who unapologetically linked the preservation of our nation during World War II with the preservation of our religion.

A BRIEF HISTORY OF THE FRANKLIN DELANO ROOSEVELT MEMORIAL

The FDR Memorial was completed only very recently in 1997, although planning for the monument dates back to 1955, just ten years after FDR's death. The site for the monument along the Tidal Basin was chosen in 1959. When plans for the memorial came to a standstill in the 1960s, a simple memorial was erected, according to FDR's own modest specifications. He requested a memorial no larger than a desk with a

President Franklin Delano Roosevelt, FDR Memorial

simple inscription—"In Memory of. . ."—to be placed in front of the National Archives. In fact, this small memorial still exists today in the northwest corner by the National Archives on Pennsylvania Avenue.

After numerous design competitions, architect John Halperin's proposal for the monument was finally selected in 1978. Halperin's design is distinctly different from the other prominent memorials on the National Mall, as it depicts not just Roosevelt the president, but guides visitors through the Great Depression and World War II era. It stands in stark contrast to the compact Lincoln, Jefferson, and Washington memorials, offering visitors a tour through each of FDR's four terms on a meandering path of marble and granite. Included with the memorial are numerous waterfalls and trees that form much of the monument's boundary alongside the Tidal Basin.

Halperin constructed four open-air "rooms" with a collection of quotes, statues, and reliefs. Each "room" depicts one of FDR's four terms. Halperin's design allows visitors to catch a glimpse of the adversity the nation faced during FDR's presidency, which encompassed some of the most trying times in American history.

FDR's first term, from 1932–1936, occurred during the throes of the Great Depression, a time of widespread economic and social dislocation. With up to 30 percent of Americans unemployed at the time, FDR inherited an economy in chaos and a demoralized nation. In his first term, FDR sought to follow through on his promise of a "new deal" for the American people. The New Deal, as it came to be known, was comprised of a series of social and employment programs, which, although failing to end the Depression, provided at the very least a necessary morale boost to thousands of previously unemployed workers. FDR urged Americans to "choose the path . . . of faith . . . love . . . and hope toward our fellow man."

FDR's next term saw the world come to the precipice of global conflict as Japan continued to expand its invasion of China and Germany seized the Sudetenland in Czechoslovakia. Here, in the "room" for the second term, a sculpture depicts a man listening intently to a radio. Throughout this troubled time, FDR spoke with the nation in a series of "fireside chats" over the radio. These fireside chats provided FDR a medium to communicate with a distressed population, allowing him to form a personal connection with millions of Americans. FDR's addresses were well suited to his affable personality and soothing persona. World War II in Europe began in earnest in 1939, with Hitler's invasion of

Depression Bread Line, FDR Memorial, 1991 by George Segal. ©The George and Helen Segal Foundation/Licensed by VAGA, New York, NY

Poland, and the United States increased its assistance to Western democracies, providing everything short of armed soldiers.

The tumultuous years of FDR's third term, 1940–1944, are marked in the memorial by a series of large granite stones obstructing the visitor's path. A loud waterfall symbolizes the violence of the war years. After the Japanese attack on Pearl Harbor in 1941, America plunged into the Second World War, leading the Allies to victory over the Axis powers in 1945. Although he was reelected in 1944, FDR died after serving only a few weeks of his fourth term. Among the most controversial aspects of the memorial is the depiction of FDR in a wheelchair. The president, who suffered from the crippling effects of polio, made scant mention of his debilitating illness and refused to be seen publicly in his wheelchair. Supporters of this imagery have argued that depicting FDR in a wheelchair is a testament to the progress we have made as a nation in better understanding and embracing those with physical limitations, as FDR feared that appearing in a wheelchair in public would have conveyed weakness.

First Lady Eleanor Roosevelt, FDR Memorial

FAITH AND THE FDR MEMORIAL

The recently constructed FDR Memorial is noticeably devoid of references to our Creator, despite Roosevelt's obvious conviction of the importance of the nation's belief in God during the war. However, faith is mentioned in two areas.

To the right of the first waterfall, you can see this inscription:

> In these days of difficulty, we Americans everywhere must and shall choose the path of social justice . . . the path of faith, the path of hope, and the path of love toward our fellow man.

As you leave the memorial, the last quotation on the wall reads: "Freedom of speech; Freedom of worship; Freedom from want; Freedom from fear." These words are taken from Roosevelt's 1941 State of the Union address and show the value he placed on our nation's religious liberty. Many are more familiar with this FDR quote from the four Norman Rockwell paintings inspired by Roosevelt's speech.

Four Freedoms, FDR Memorial

THE FAITH OF
FRANKLIN ROOSEVELT

As Professor Gary S. Smith has observed, Franklin Roosevelt often "stressed the importance of spiritual renewal, faith, and social justice and urged Americans to work to achieve a more robust spiritual life." It may surprise many to learn that after the Allies successfully took Normandy Beach, Roosevelt led the American people in prayer in a nationwide radio address:

Almighty God, our sons, pride of our nation, this day have set upon a mighty endeavor, a struggle to preserve our republic, our religion, and our civilizations, and to set free a suffering humanity.

He used the occasion to commit the American people to a rededication of their faith:

Many people have urged that I call the nation into a single day of special prayer. But because the road is long and the desire is great, I ask that our people devote themselves in a continuance of prayer. As we rise to each new day, and again when each day is spent, let words of prayer be on our lips, invoking Thy help to our efforts.

Roosevelt knew how our faith bound us together as a country:

And, O Lord, give us faith. Give us faith in Thee; faith in our sons; faith in each other; faith in our united crusade. Let not the keenness of our spirit ever be dulled. Let not the impacts of temporary events, of temporal matters of but a fleeting moment, let not these deter us in our unconquerable purpose. Thy will be done, Almighty God. Amen.

This address is so powerful that we launched a project in 2006 to encourage radio stations across the country to air FDR's D-Day prayer on June 6. Our goal was to remind America that the most successful liberal president of the twentieth century led an entire nation in prayer for the safety of our troops. Thanks to a great deal of support, more than 1,000 stations have aired FDR's prayer over the last three years. We hope next year you will join us in asking your local radio stations to air FDR's D-Day prayer.

Roosevelt's faith was very important to him well before the war. He was a member of the Episcopal Church, serving as senior warden of the St. James Church in New York throughout his presidency. Furthermore, as Professor Smith notes, in 1935 he sought "council and advice" on the impact of domestic policy from the many clergymen whom he invited to the White House.

Roosevelt's faith became most important when he needed to rally the American people to defend western civilization against fascism. Even before Pearl Harbor, he recognized the threat that the Nazis and Japanese posed to our religious freedoms.

On May 27, 1941, Roosevelt spoke to the nation in one of his many radio addresses, to announce a state of "Unlimited National Emergency." He accurately described the "Nazi world" as one that "does not recognize any God except Hitler . . . as ruthless as the Communists in the denial of God . . . where moral standards are measured by treachery and bribery." He recognized that this posed an impending global conflict "between human slavery and human freedom—between pagan brutality and the

Christian ideal." America, he explained, shall side with "human freedom—which is the Christian ideal" and will only accept "a world consecrated to freedom of speech and expression—freedom of every person to worship God in his own way—freedom from want—and freedom from terror."

Roosevelt affirmed that such success could only be obtained through a combined faith in freedom and God. He called on Americans to "reassert our abiding faith in the vitality of our constitutional republic as a perpetual home of freedom, of tolerance, and of devotion to the word of God." Roosevelt then concluded by quoting the Founding Fathers, who faced similar odds "with a firm reliance on the protection of Divine Providence."

Roosevelt again addressed the nation by radio as war became ever more inevitable, to express to Americans the threat Nazism posed to our democratic and religious freedoms. On October 27, 1941, he described a German document outlining Hitler's plan to "abolish all existing religions" in which "the property of all churches will be seized by the Reich and its puppets. The cross and all other symbols of religion are to be forbidden . . . in place of the cross of Christ will be put two symbols—the swastika and the naked sword." Roosevelt then concluded with a pledge to the Nazis that "We stand ready in the defense of our nation and the faith of our fathers to do what God has given us the power to see as our full duty."

Franklin Roosevelt was a man of deep religious belief who understood, just as powerfully as Washington before him, that religion and morality were indispensable supports to the preservation of our liberties and our country.

IN GOD WE TRUST

The U.S. Capitol Building

"The foundation of our society and our government rest so much on the teachings of the Bible that it would be difficult to support them if faith in these teachings would cease to be practically universal in our country."

CALVIN COOLIDGE
Thirtieth President of the United States

Chapter 7

THE CAPITOL BUILDING

United States Capitol

Thus far, we've seen examples of how our greatest leaders drew upon their faith in our Creator both for strength and guidance to lead this country. It only makes sense that they would design a Capitol that would reflect this same source of inspiration.

A BRIEF HISTORY OF THE
U.S. CAPITOL BUILDING

Like no other building in Washington, the Capitol defines the skyline of the District of Columbia, the great white dome standing as the most prominent structure in the city, with only the Washington Monument reaching higher. Like many other historic buildings in Washington, D.C., its history is fraught with controversy, halting construction, and of course, political maneuvering.

The man who laid out Washington's broad diagonal avenues and picturesque but frustrating traffic circles, Pierre L'Enfant, was also originally given the task of designing the Capitol. L'Enfant, however, refused to submit his ideas for the building in blueprint form, insisting that his design could only be cognitively constructed. His intransigence led to his dismissal in 1792, and led the commission to accept Dr. William Thornton's design. President George Washington laid the cornerstone for the Capitol in 1793, beginning a long and cumbersome construction process. The north wing of the Capitol was ready for Congress to move into by 1800.

Construction on the Capitol would not begin again until 1803, this time under the auspices of architect Benjamin Henry Latrobe. Latrobe changed much of Thornton's original design, simplifying much of the construction plan, while adding extra space for committee rooms and office spaces in the south wing. In addition, Latrobe rebuilt much of the north wing of the Capitol. By the end of the decade, war with Great Britain loomed on the horizon, and Latrobe was unable to complete construction of the south wing. The two wings were connected by only a wooden walkway as the War of 1812 began. The British invasion of Washington in 1814 resulted in the partial destruction of the Capitol on August 25, although a fortuitous rainstorm saved the building from being completely burned to the ground.

Latrobe resumed work on the Capitol in 1815, although he resigned after heavy—and often unfair—criticism of construction delays. Boston architect Charles Bulfinch was designated as Latrobe's replacement in 1818. Bulfinch oversaw the completion of the north and south wings (including a chamber for the Supreme Court). Following Bulfinch's departure in 1830, incremental improvements were made to the structure's interior, such as running water. The Capitol's original designers, however, had failed to envision the Union's seemingly ever-expanding number of states and representatives, and by 1850, the Capitol was quickly becoming overcrowded.

President Millard Fillmore chose Thomas Walter to continue the Capitol's construction and rehabilitation. Work generally progressed on schedule under Walter's tenure, and the House was able to meet in its new chambers (presently Statuary Hall) by the end of 1857, while the Senate chamber's completion was only two years away. As the nation was thrust into the bitter throes of the Civil War, construction on the Capitol was again halted. The nation's Capitol building—as well as its home city—was forced to endure the bloody realities of a nation divided. The Capitol provided soldiers a makeshift barracks, hospital, and bakery. Despite the war, construction resumed in 1862, and aesthetic improvements to the inside continued as Constantino Brumidi finished *The Apotheosis of Washington* along the canopy fresco on the inside of the Rotunda in 1866.

President George Washington in the United States Capitol Rotunda

Now that the structure of the building itself was mostly complete, modernization of the building's heating and cooling systems was undertaken through the end of the century. Work was also continued on the Capitol grounds. Other major projects on the Capitol have included the extension of the East Front, in addition to a restoration project of the West Front. Those fortunate enough to have visited the Capitol before September 11, 2001, will recall the spectacular view of the city provided from the steps of the West Front. Sadly, locals and tourists alike are now deprived of this inspiring view due to new security restrictions. A new visitor's center was finally completed in 2008.

RELIGIOUS IMAGERY IN THE CAPITOL

The U.S. Capitol Building is filled with religious imagery and inscriptions. As you walk up the steps of the Capitol, recall that on September 12, 2001, two hundred members of Congress gathered on these steps to sing "God Bless America." In a similar scene in June 2002, members of the House of Representatives gathered here to recite the Pledge of Allegiance after the Ninth Circuit Court ruled that it was unconstitutional to describe our nation as "under God," which, of course, was exactly the way Washington described our nation in July 1776 and Lincoln at Gettysburg in 1863.

Today, the House and Senate both open their daily sessions with the Pledge of Allegiance. Representative Sonny Montgomery (a Democrat from Mississippi) recited the first Pledge of Allegiance on the House floor on September 13, 1988. Former Speaker of the House Jim Wright decided to make the Pledge a daily ritual, and in 1995, the House rules were amended to make it permanent. The Senate has never officially made the Pledge a permanent feature, but it has recited it before each session since June 24, 1999.

Upon entering the Rotunda, you will be immediately struck by the religious imagery. Eight different historical paintings are on display. Pay particular attention to a few. First, the painting *The Landing of Columbus* depicts his arrival on the shores of America. Columbus later said he was convinced to sail because "it was the Lord who put it into my mind" and that "the Gospel must still be preached to so many lands."

The Embarkation of the Pilgrims, United States Capitol

Second, on the south side of the Rotunda, between statues of Martin Luther King, Jr., and President Dwight Eisenhower, is a painting titled *The Embarkation of the Pilgrims,* by Robert W. Weir, from 1843. This depicts the deck of the ship *Speedwell* as it departed for the New World from Delft Haven, Holland, on July 22, 1620. You will see that the Pilgrims are observing a day of prayer and fasting, led by William Brewster, who is holding a Bible, and John Robertson, a pastor. The rainbow at the left side of the painting symbolizes hope and divine protection.

Third, the painting *The Discovery of the Mississippi* may be found directly next to *The Embarkation of the Pilgrims.* This painting shows Spanish explorer Hernando DeSoto's encounter with the Native Americans. DeSoto was the first European to set foot in what is now Mississippi. On the right side of the painting, a monk prays as a crucifix is planted into the ground. DeSoto's burial is also depicted in the frieze that goes around the Rotunda. This is identifiable by a priest making the sign of a cross over DeSoto's body, covered by a sheet.

Finally, the painting *The Baptism of Pocahontas* demonstrates the baptism of one of the first converts in the Virginia colony. Directly overhead is *The Apotheosis of Washington,* which depicts our first president's ascent into heaven. The thirteen maidens surrounding him symbolize the original thirteen states.

At the ground level of the Rotunda, a glass case can be found that holds a gold replica of the Magna Carta. This was a gift from the British government in 1976. Many of the first travelers to what would become the colonies came with a copy of this document in hand. It was later used to justify the colonialists' protests against the Stamp Act and other violations of their rights. In fact, the seal adopted by Massachusetts on the eve of the revolution featured a militiaman with a sword in one hand and a copy of the Magna Carta in the other.

Various inscriptions around the Capitol demonstrate the reliance of our country on God and faith. In the Cox Corridor in the House wing of the Capitol, a line from "America the Beautiful" is carved into the wall: "America! God shed His grace on thee, and crown thy good

The Baptism of Pocahontas, United States Capitol

The Apotheosis of George Washington, United States Capitol

with brotherhood, from sea to shining sea!" Also in the House chamber is the inscription "In God We Trust." At the east entrance to the Senate chamber, the words *Annuit Coeptis* are inscribed, Latin for "God has favored our undertakings." The words "In God We Trust" are also written over the southern entrance. "What hath God Wrought!," the first message sent over the telegraph, is inscribed on the Samuel F. B. Morse Plaque found outside of the old Supreme Court Chamber in the Capitol.

In the House chamber, above the central Gallery door, stands a marble relief of Moses, the greatest of twenty-three noted law-givers (and the only one full-faced). Statues of many early leaders are displayed throughout the Capitol Building. Most of these leaders were Christians, and many were ministers, including George Washington, James Garfield, Samuel Adams, Reverend Peter Muhlenberg, Reverend Roger Williams, Reverend Marcus Whitman, Daniel Webster, Lew Wallace, Reverend Jason Lee, John Winthrop, Reverend Jonathan Trumbull, Roger Sherman, and Francis Willard.

THE CAPITOL CHAPEL

Unfortunately, the Capitol Building Chapel is off limits to all but members of Congress and their guests. However, its history is instructive. The chapel was built after a particularly powerful display of God's role in American public life.

Throughout American history, presidents have called for national days of prayer to pay tribute and give thanks. In 1952, Congress issued a joint resolution calling for a prayer service on the steps of the Capitol. The service was conducted by the Reverend Billy Graham. Thousands

Stained Glass Window, Chapel, United States Capitol

of people came to the service in the pouring February rain. After this display, Congress called for the construction of a room "with facilities for prayer and meditation, for use of the members of the Senate and House of Representatives."

Found in the Capitol's Chapel is a stained-glass window depicting George Washington in prayer, under the inscription "This Nation Under God." Furthermore, a prayer is inscribed in the window. It says, "Preserve me, God, for in Thee do I put my trust."

CHURCH SERVICES IN THE CAPITOL

As mentioned earlier in chapter 3 regarding the Thomas Jefferson Memorial, the United States Capitol held church services well before the construction of the chapel in the 1950s. At the time of the building's construction, there were no churches in the District of Columbia to serve the needs of members of Congress and the president. Therefore, such services were held in the Capitol.

Thomas Jefferson attended these services throughout his terms as vice president and president, which were often conducted by his friend Reverend John Leland. Ironically, Jefferson attended one such service just two days after he wrote his famous response to the Danbury Baptists Association of Connecticut in which he referred to a "wall of separation" between church and state. President Jefferson clearly understood that his "wall of separation" would allow his attending church services in the U.S. Capitol without even the appearance of the state either establishing a national church or imposing a religious belief system on the people.

James Madison, who is widely considered to be the author of the

Religion Clauses of the First Amendment, also attended these church services in the Capitol. In fact, while Congress was debating the language of the First Amendment, they were also working to pass legislation to hire and pay for official House and Senate chaplains. Accordingly, Madison clearly saw no conflict between favoring religious observances in public spaces and opposing an official national religion.

STATUES OF RELIGIOUS LEADERS

Just south of the Rotunda is a semicircular chamber known as Statuary Hall. This room was originally built for the House of Representatives in 1807, who met here for nearly fifty years. Its original purpose, however, was short lived.

British troops destroyed the room when they ransacked Washington, D.C., in the War of 1812. When the chamber's reconstruction was completed in 1819, members of Congress found that the curved ceiling easily carried sound from one side of the room to the other. This made it possible to clearly hear conversations across the room. Obviously, the members found it difficult to conduct business in this environment. Within a few decades, the House constructed and moved into a new chamber which is still in use today.

In 1864, the House voted to change the name and purpose of this room. The chamber became known as National Statuary Hall. Each state was invited to send two statues of prominent citizens to be displayed here. As the number of states grew, so did the number of statues. Today, every state has contributed two statues to the Capitol. Thirty-five statues are displayed in Statuary Hall, while the others are dispersed throughout the Capitol.

Father James Marquette, United States Capitol

Several states have chosen to highlight religious leaders. Below are a few examples:

Father Marquette—Wisconsin

Jacques Marquette was a French Jesuit missionary and explorer who, along with his companion, Louis Jolliet, embarked upon an exploration of the Mississippi River in 1673. With help from Native Americans, Marquette and Jolliet discovered that the Mississippi River flowed into the Gulf of Mexico and not the Pacific Ocean, as previously rumored. In 1674, Marquette established a mission in Kaskaskia, Illinois. His statue stands in a corridor near the House of Representatives as a gift from the state of Wisconsin.

Brigham Young—Utah

Brigham Young was the famous Mormon leader who led his followers west to Utah. Young joined the Church of Jesus Christ of Latter-day Saints in 1832 and helped establish several Mormon towns in Ohio and Illinois. Young quickly became a leader of the church, and by 1844 rose to the presidency. Due mostly to religious persecution, he set out with approximately 150 followers and founded Salt Lake City, Utah. Soon, the city was populated with thousands of Mormons who came from all over the country. Young's statue stands in Statuary Hall.

Junipero Serra—California

Father Junipero Serra was born in Mallorca, Spain in 1713 and became a leading missionary in America. In 1769 he established his first mission in San Diego and proceeded to establish eight others, including missions in San Buenaventura, San Carlos, San Francisco de Assisi, San Gabriel,

Father Junipero Serra's Cross, United States Capitol

San Juan Capistrano, San Luis Obispo, and Santa Clara. Father Serra tirelessly sought to convert Native Americans to Christianity. His statue was submitted to the Capitol in 1931 by the state of California and can be found in Statuary Hall.

Father Damien—Hawaii

Father Damien was ordained a priest at the age of 24 in the Cathedral of Our Lady of Peace in Honolulu. After traveling to a leper colony in Hawaii, he decided to spend his life ministering to the infected and trying to alleviate their pain. Father Damien relocated the settlement on the island of Molokai and built numerous chapels and orphanages. Here, he helped treat the sick before succumbing to the disease himself. He is known today as the "Apostle of Lepers," and is expected to be canonized in October 2009. His statue can be found in the Hall of Columns.

WE ARE A RELIGIOUS PEOPLE

The Supreme Court

"The American nation from its first settlement at Jamestown to this hour is based upon and permeated by the principles of the Bible."

JUSTICE DAVID JOSEPH BREWER

(1837-1910)
Supreme Court Justice

Chapter 8

THE SUPREME COURT

United States Supreme Court

While recent years have seen increasing hostility from the courts to public displays of religion, the Supreme Court itself is filled with them. In fact, if you have the chance to sit in on a hearing, notice that all sessions begin with the Court's Marshal announcing: "God save the United States and this honorable court."

The truth is that throughout most of our history, the decisions of the Supreme Court have recognized the fact that we are a religious nation. For example, in the 1952 case *Zorach vs. Clauson,* the Court upheld a statute that allowed students to be released from school to attend religious classes. Justice William O. Douglas wrote:

> We are a religious people and our institutions presuppose a supreme being. When the state encourages religious instruction or cooperates with religious authorities by adjusting the schedule of public events to sectarian needs, it follows the best of our traditions. We cannot read into the Bill of Rights a philosophy of hostility to religion.

A BRIEF HISTORY OF THE SUPREME COURT

The Supreme Court has only recently had a building exclusively for itself. When the federal government was relocated to the District of Columbia in 1800, Congress had allotted no building or space for the Court, so it shared space in the Capitol building, jumping from room to room. (The Court even met once in a private home during the War of 1812.) Finally, the Court settled in the Old Senate Chamber from 1860 until 1935.

Compared with other well-known structures and monuments in Washington, D.C., the building of the Supreme Court proceeded with remarkably little controversy or delay. Construction began in 1932 and was completed in 1935, and the project cost under $10 million. It was

Supreme Court Chief Justice William Howard Taft (who served as president from 1909 until 1913) who persuaded Congress to authorize a building entirely for the Supreme Court. Taft selected Cass Gilbert to design the building, which is modeled in familiar Corinthian style. Gilbert's use of Greek and Roman architecture—chosen because they manifest democratic principles—is ironic because Cass's friendship with the fascist leader, Benito Mussolini, allowed him to obtain marble for the Court's construction. Gilbert also used marble from quarries across the states: Vermont marble for the Court's exterior; Georgia marble for the inner courtyards; and Alabama marble on the upper floors in corridors and entrance hallways.

Both Gilbert and Taft died before the Court's completion in 1935, although Gilbert's son, Cass Gilbert, Jr., would complete his father's work. In a fashion unfamiliar to Washington, the cost of building the Supreme Court was less than originally appropriated for the task, and nearly $100,000 was returned to the Treasury upon completion of the building.

RELIGIOUS IMAGERY IN THE SUPREME COURT

The most striking religious imagery at the Supreme Court is that of Moses with the Ten Commandments. Affirming the Judeo-Christian roots of our legal system, Moses can be found in several places: in the center of the East Pediment on 2nd Street NE, as a relief on the southwest corner of the building on 1st Street NE, inside the Upper Great Hall, and inside the actual courtroom as part of the "great lawgivers of history" frieze.

Mohammad, the prophet of Islam, is also depicted in this frieze. While meditating in a cave outside of Mecca—now Islam's holiest city—Mohammed experienced a vision of the archangel Gabriel. Gabriel told him that he had been chosen as a prophet of God and instructed him to recite publicly verses he had been offered during the vision. These revelations continued, and Mohammed gradually gained a larger group of followers. The verses came to be known collectively as the Qu'ran, and Mohammed sought to spread his teachings.

Next to the sculpted depiction of Mohammed is one of Charlemagne, regarded by scholars as the greatest king of the Middle Ages. During a period of European history known for small, warring kingdoms continually rife with sectarian disputes, Charlemagne bucked this trend, uniting much of Western Europe under his rule. He is credited with temporarily restoring a decaying Western Europe after the fall of the Roman Empire, as his rule fostered a wellspring of literature, art, and academic study, all of which had been in steep decline. Referred to as the Carolingian Renaissance, Charlemagne's court specifically promoted such cultural development, and Charlemagne himself even managed to learn to read, a highly atypical feat for kings at the time. Charlemagne's empire would be divided among his three grandsons upon his death, ending a brief span of a mostly united Western Europe.

Even more important than the cultural and political revival that Charlemagne's empire helped to bring back, his legacy would entrench the Roman Catholic Church politically in Europe for centuries. Recognized as the head of the church in his domains, Charlemagne converted conquered peoples to Christianity, most notably the pagans of Saxony. He also firmly established the Church's position of prominence within the

Confucius, Moses, and Solon, United States Supreme Court

kingdoms of Europe, a move that would solidify religion as an influential social and political force in Europe for centuries to come.

Along the East Pediment of the Supreme Court is a sculpture entitled "Justice the Guardian of Liberty," which features Moses at the center, flanked by Solon and Confucius. Cass Gilbert, the chief architect of the project, allowed his sculptor, Herman A. McNeil, considerable discretion in choosing his subjects. Thus McNeil chose Moses, Solon, and

Confucius because they represented three great civilizations to the East, from which "Law . . . was naturally and normally derived or inherited."

Although the story of Moses is well known to most visitors of the Court, fewer are familiar with Solon and Confucius. A renowned Athenian legislator, Solon was best known for first instituting trial by jury and for his success in writing a constitution for the Greek city of Attica, which had endured chaos before Solon's constitution. Later, as a leader of Athens, Solon implemented a number of political and economic reforms that prevented the lower classes from losing their quickly eroding rights. Solon went on to repeal most of the brutal punishments for crimes codified by the Athenian lawmaker Draco, whose name today still bears reference to the nature of the severe penalties he enforced. Through such actions, Solon is credited with preventing the advent of complete oligarchy in Athens and with restoring many of the rights of the lower class.

Confucius was a great philosopher and thinker of feudal China. Many compare his tremendous influence on Chinese history to that of Socrates' effect on the West. A frustrated low-level bureaucrat disillusioned by his inability to change the policy of the prince he worked for, Confucius resigned his position and set out on a journey across China to preach his political and social philosophies to China's many rulers. Much like Europe's Middle Ages, during Confucius's life (551–479 BC), China was a collection of small states vying for power. Confucius was convinced that he could eventually bring this state of disorder to an end. Although he ultimately failed, his teachings still influence Eastern thought today. Stressing the need for men to live their lives within the parameters of heaven, Confucius taught that leaders should govern by their own example, with care and concern for the ruled. He also stressed the idea that government should rule based on the people's natural morality and emphasized the principles of self-discipline and personal responsibility for one's actions.

THE ROCK
UPON WHICH OUR
REPUBLIC RESTS

The Library of Congress

*"The highest story of the
American Revolution is this:
It connected in one indissoluble bond
the principles of civil government
with the principles of Christianity."*

JOHN ADAMS
Second President of the United States

Chapter 9

THE LIBRARY OF CONGRESS

The Great Hall, Library of Congress

The Library of Congress was originally established in 1800 as a legislative library. However, it grew into much more.

Today on its website, www.loc.gov, the Library of Congress immodestly describes its mission "to make its resources available and useful to the Congress and the American people and to sustain and preserve a universal collection of knowledge and creativity for future generations."

To accomplish this monumental mission, the Library of Congress employs over 5,000 people and houses approximately 130 million items catalogued on approximately 530 miles of bookshelves. This includes over 29 million books and other printed materials, 2.7 million recordings, 12 million photographs, 4.8 million maps, and 58 million manuscripts, with 10,000 new items added to the collection daily (out of over 22,000 submissions daily).

The Library of Congress simultaneously serves as a legislative library and research arm of Congress, the copyright agency of the United States, a center for scholarship offering research material in more than 450 languages, a public institution open to everyone over high school age, a government library for the executive branch and cabinet agencies, a law library, the home of the nation's poet laureate, and the sponsor of cultural programs and exhibitions of national and international scope.

All this makes the Library of Congress by far the largest library in the world.

Most of these 10,000 new items a day are received as a result of the copyright submission process by the U.S. Copyright Office. Others are purchased by Congress or received as gifts from individuals or other government agencies. The rest are obtained through a library exchange program that trades the unwanted submitted items to other libraries in the United States and abroad for items the Library of Congress needs. The items not selected are then given to other federal agencies or donated to educational institutions and tax-exempt charities.

The Library of Congress also houses THOMAS. Named for Thomas Jefferson, THOMAS is the way in which any citizen can access the Internet and read any bill online that is before Congress. Access was granted to the public during the first days of the 104th Congress in 1995 after I was sworn in as Speaker of the House of Representatives. Providing the public with access to information about the business of Congress was one of my proudest accomplishments as Speaker.

A BRIEF HISTORY
OF THE LIBRARY OF CONGRESS

The early years of the Library of Congress were tumultuous. On August 24, 1814, just fourteen years after it was founded, the Library and its collection of 3,000 volumes were burnt to the ground when British troops torched the Capitol building in which the Library was originally housed. Thanks to Thomas Jefferson, Congress was able to quickly establish a new, even larger collection. Jefferson agreed to sell his personal library of 6,487 books to Congress for $23,950 to "recommence" its library. Tragically, many of these volumes were lost when, on Christmas Eve 1851, another fire destroyed two-thirds of the collection.

Despite this loss, the purchase of Jefferson's collection set the future course for the Library of Congress. Over six thousand books did more than restock the Library's shelves; it expanded its collection from largely legislative works to include books on architecture, the arts, science, literature, and geography. It was Jefferson's collection, and, therefore, his eclectic interests and tastes, which first planted the seed of the

Library of Congress' current, expansive mission as a "universal collection of knowledge and creativity."

Not surprisingly, it takes three buildings on Capitol Hill to hold a library with such an audacious mission. The Library eventually migrated from the Capitol to the newly constructed Thomas Jefferson Building in 1897. It was joined with the John Adams Building in 1938 and the James Madison Memorial Building in 1981 so as to have room to store the Library of Congress' massive collection.

In 1924, the nation's two most precious documents, the Declaration of Independence and the Constitution, were put on permanent public display in a specially designed "shrine" in the Great Hall of the Jefferson Building. The Library transferred both documents to the National Archives in 1952, but retains as one of its greatest treasures Jefferson's handwritten draft of the Declaration of Independence.

THE GREAT HALL

Out of the over one hundred thirty million items in the Library of Congress' collection, only two are on permanent display in the Great Hall. The first is the Giant Bible of Mainz, a handwritten and illustrated version of the Bible considered to be one of the most beautiful ever created. The second is the Gutenberg Bible, the first mass printed book, which soon made hand-printed books like the Giant Bible of Mainz obsolete. The copy at the Library of Congress is printed on vellum, or animal skin, and is one of only three perfect copies still in existence.

These two artifacts were produced within two years of each other in the same small town of Mainz, Germany. Two contradictory theories about their creation are widely repeated in the academic world. The first is that in an ironic twist of fate, the Giant Bible of Mainz was the model upon which Johannes Gutenberg based his typeset. The second is that the two creators of the works are said to have no knowledge of the other's existence. The great works were reunited when Lawrence J. Rosenwald donated the Giant Bible of Mainz to the Library of Congress on April 4, 1952, the 500th anniversary of its completion.

The Gutenberg Bible, The Great Hall, Library of Congress

Johannes Gutenberg was not the first to invent printing. The Chinese used printing techniques with wood typeset centuries earlier. However, Gutenberg was the first to invent a practical way to mass produce individual pieces of type in metal as well as invent a form of ink that would not smudge on metal. This made Johannes Gutenberg's invention much more durable and replicable than anything else in the world.

It is hard to overestimate the impact of the printing press upon the world. Until Gutenberg's invention, all books had to be hand-transcribed. It took years to produce just one copy of the Bible, making the printed word a luxury afforded by only the very rich. Johannes Gutenberg was able to press hundreds of copies of the Bible in little more than a year.

Within fifty years, Gutenberg's printing press had been copied and refined in cities all across Europe. By the early sixteenth century, the entire collection of Western "classical" knowledge had been printed and mass produced. This mass production and distribution of knowledge allowed philosophers and scientists to easily share information for the first time, paving the way for the Renaissance and scientific revolution. It was the chief tool that allowed what we now describe as "Western" values to spread across Europe and eventually the North American continent.

It is no accident that this process began with the printing of a Bible, the foundation upon which the pillars of our society rest.

In addition to the two Bibles, the Great Hall displays other evidence of the nation's strong religious underpinnings. The following passages are inscribed on the ceiling and the walls of the Great Hall: "The light shineth in darkness, and the darkness comprehendeth it not" (John 1:5); "Wisdom is the principal thing; therefore, get wisdom and with all thy getting, get understanding" (Proverbs 4:7); and Dante's "Nature is the Art of God."

THE MAIN READING ROOM

Anyone who wishes access to the Library of Congress's books and bound periodicals must first start in the Main Reading Room. Here researchers begin their initial search for knowledge using the electronic resources in the Computer Catalog Center and the Main Card Catalog. Approximately 70,000 volumes are stored in the Main Reading Room reference collection and hundreds of books and bound periodicals are delivered to the Main Reading Room every day for research.

There are several instances of religious imagery and scripture verse

Main Reading Room, Library of Congress

found in the Main Reading Room. They include a bronze statue of Moses holding the Ten Commandments and a painting on the ceiling called *Judea*, showing a young Jewish woman praying.

Judea, Main Reading Room, Library of Congress

In addition, two scripture passages are inscribed on the walls: "What doth the Lord require of thee, but to do justly, and to love mercy, and to walk humbly with thy God" (Micah 6:8) and "The heavens declare the Glory of God, and the firmament showeth His handiwork" (Psalm 19:1).

Micah 6:8, Main Reading Room, Library of Congress

"RELIGION AND THE FOUNDING OF THE AMERICAN REPUBLIC"

In 1998, the Library of Congress held an exhibit called "Religion and the Founding of the American Republic." The exhibit explored the role of religion in the colonies from Jamestown through the post-Revolutionary War era in which many of our governmental and societal institutions were formed. While no longer on display, this exhibit continues to influence thinking about the role of religion in the founding of our great nation.

The exhibit displayed over two hundred artifacts from the founding of the American Republic. This included manuscripts, books, correspondence, and paintings both from the Library's collection and on loan from other institutions. The exhibit was divided into seven sections focusing on the following issues:

- America as a refuge for those seeking freedom from religious persecution in Europe and how their beliefs formed the foundation for our society;
- The Great Awakening from 1740 to 1745 and how it led to the drive to Independence;
- The role of religion in the lives of our nation's greatest Revolutionary leaders;
- The way religion affected those who formed the structure of our government;
- The policies of our early federal government leaders toward religion;
- The policies of our early state government leaders toward religion; and
- The "Golden Age" of Evangelicalism in America through the 1830s.

The exhibits demonstrated with conviction that religion and morality were, in Alexis de Tocqueville's words, "indispensable to the maintenance of republican institutions."

I hope that those who left the exhibit asked themselves the following question: "Are the religious and moral supports described by George Washington no longer as important to our nation's well-being? Or do we ban the expression of such supports in our public square at the peril of our Republic?"

IN GOD I TRUST

The Ronald Reagan Building

*"Faith and religion play a critical role
in the political life of our nation—
and always have—and that the church—
and by that I mean all churches,
all denominations—have had a
strong influence on the state."*

RONALD REAGAN
Fortieth President of the United States

Chapter 10

THE RONALD REAGAN BUILDING

Liberty of Worship, Ronald Reagan Building and International Trade Center

Ronald Reagan spoke eloquently and often about his faith in God and how He inspired him and the nation. In 1984, he wrote *In God I Trust*, a memoir of his life and faith. On March 8, 1983, he declared the following in an address to an evangelical convention:

I tell you there are a great many God-fearing, dedicated, noble men and women in public life, present company included. And yes, we need your help to keep us ever mindful of the ideas and the principles that brought us into the public arena in the first place. The basis of those ideals and principles is a commitment to freedom and personal liberty that, itself, is grounded in the much deeper realization that freedom prospers only where the blessings of God are avidly sought and humbly accepted. The American experiment in democracy rests on this insight.

A BRIEF HISTORY OF THE RONALD REAGAN BUILDING

The Ronald Reagan Building and International Trade Center holds the distinction of being the first federal building designed to be used by both the government and private sector. The land on which it rests was first purchased by the federal government in the 1920s, but it remained undeveloped through the Great Depression because of funding constraints. The only exception was a memorial fountain to Oscar S. Straus. Straus was a diplomat and the Secretary of Commerce and Labor from 1906 through 1909 (Commerce and Labor were split into two departments in 1913).

The Straus Fountain can still be seen today, along with several statues and other artworks surrounding the outside of the building. The Ronald Reagan Building and International Trade Center was designed by the firm of Pei, Cobb, Fred and Partners. Dedicated in 1998, it covers more than seven acres and houses nearly seven thousand federal employees, along with private sector, non-profit, and international trade organizations. It was also the venue for the fiftieth anniversary summit of the North Atlantic Treaty Organization (NATO) in April 1999.

The Ronald Reagan Building and International Trade Center also houses the Washington, D.C. Visitor Information Center, a useful spot to find more information on what to see while in our nation's capital.

Outside the main entrance to the building is a statue called "Liberty of Worship." The figure is shown as leaning against the Ten Commandments, yet another allusion to the close tie between religion and liberty. The inscription on the statue states: "Our liberty of worship is not a concession nor a privilege but an inherent right."

THE FAITH OF RONALD REAGAN

It is especially appropriate that the "Liberty of Worship" statue is found outside a federal building named after Ronald Reagan. President Reagan saw religious liberty as an irreplaceable underpinning of our democratic freedoms. This theme can be seen in many of his speeches as president.

In a speech at Georgetown University on its bicentennial, Reagan commended the theme of the celebration: learning, faith, and freedom. "Each reinforces the others, each makes the others possible. For what are they without each other?" He asked the audience to pray that all of America be guided by learning, faith, and freedom. "De Tocqueville said it in 1835, and it's as true today as it was then: 'Despotism may govern without faith, but liberty cannot. Religion is more needed in democratic societies than in any other.'"

As president, Reagan frequently invoked the words of George Washington, who said that religion and morality were "indispensable supports" to the prosperity of our political system. During a radio address in December 1983, he described one of his favorite paintings, which shows George Washington praying at Valley Forge. He said the painting "personified a people who knew it was not enough to depend on their own courage and goodness; they must also seek help from God, their Father and their Preserver."

At an ecumenical prayer breakfast in August 1984 in Dallas, Texas, Reagan said:

> I believe that faith and religion play a critical role in the political life of our nation—and always have—and that the church—and by that I mean all churches, all denominations—has had a strong influence on the state.
>
> And this has worked to our benefit as a nation. Those who created our country—the Founding Fathers and Mothers—understood that there is a divine order which transcends the human order. They saw the state, in fact, as a form of moral order and felt that the bedrock of moral order is religion.
>
> Without God, democracy will not and cannot long endure. If we ever forget that we're one nation under God, then we will be a nation gone under.

One of Reagan's most memorable speeches was delivered before the National Association of Evangelicals in March 1983. In it, he famously called the Soviet Union an "evil empire" and promised "one day, with God's help" the world's nuclear arsenals would be totally eliminated.

In the same speech, Reagan attacked the government's "attempts to water down traditional values and even abrogate the original terms of American democracy. Freedom prospers when religion is vibrant and the rule of law under God is acknowledged."

He then closed the speech with scripture: "He giveth power to the faint; and to them that have no might He increased strength. But they that wait upon the Lord shall renew their strength; they shall mount up with wings as eagles; they shall run, and not be weary."

THE DIVINE AUTHOR
OF EVERY GOOD GIFT

The White House

"And to the same Divine Author of every
good and perfect gift [James 1:17]
we are indebted for all those privileges
and advantages, religious as well
as civil, which are so richly
enjoyed in this favored land."

JAMES MADISON

Fourth President of the United States and
Chief Architect of the Constitution

Chapter 11

THE WHITE HOUSE

The White House

The White House is the quintessential symbol of the American Presidency. It serves two important roles: first, as the private home for the president and first family; second, as the executive office of the president and his senior staff. As President Bill Clinton explained on its 200th anniversary:

> For two centuries now, Americans have looked to the White House as a symbol of leadership in times of crisis, a reassurance in times of uncertainty, of continuity in times of change, a celebration in times of joy. These walls carry the story of America. It was here at the White House that President Jefferson first unrolled maps of a bountiful continent to plan the Lewis and Clark expedition. Here that President Lincoln signed the Emancipation Proclamation freeing the slaves, some of whose ancestors have quarried the very stone from which the White House was built. Here, that President Roosevelt held the Fireside Chats, willing his nation through the Depression, then marshaling our allies through the war.

A BRIEF HISTORY OF THE WHITE HOUSE

In 1790 George Washington signed an Act of Congress declaring that the United States government would reside in a newly created district, along the banks of the Potomac River. In 1791, with the help of city planner Pierre L'Enfant, Washington then chose the site for his house, which is now 1600 Pennsylvania Avenue. L'Enfant was originally slated to be the building's designer until he was dismissed by President Washington for insubordination.

In 1792 a competition was held to determine a new architect for "President's House," which included a submission by Thomas Jefferson using a pseudonym. The competition was eventually won, however, by an Irish-born architect named James Hobson who had immigrated to the United States in 1785. L'Enfant had originally envisioned a "palace" five times larger than the house eventually built, but labor and material shortages mandated a significantly more modest design. It is widely claimed that Hobson drew his inspiration from an Anglo-Irish villa in Dublin called Leinster House, which today houses the National Parliament of Ireland.

The first cornerstone of the White House was laid in October of 1792, but President Washington never had a chance to live in it, despite overseeing much of the construction. President John Adams and his wife, First Lady Abigail Adams, became the first official occupants on November 1, 1800.

The White House has undergone many structural modifications and renovations throughout its history. President Thomas Jefferson made several changes when he became the second occupant, with the aid of architect Benjamin Henry Latrobe. In 1814, the British invaded a defenseless Washington, D.C., forcing President James Madison to flee the city. The British then torched the White House, destroying virtually the entire building except for the outer walls. As a result, Hobson was recalled to Washington to return the White House to its prior state. Many of the building's carved ornamentation were reused in the process, despite bearing scorch marks from the fire. In 1824, Hobson completed the south portico. Six years later, President Andrew Jackson oversaw the construction of the north portico.

Over the course of the nineteenth century the White House was modified under successive presidents to embrace new technology. Running water was introduced by Andrew Jackson in 1833. In 1848, James Polk replaced candlelight with gas light. In 1879, the first White House telephone was connected for Rutherford B. Hayes. And in 1891, President and Mrs. Benjamin Harrison installed electric wiring.

Under President Theodore Roosevelt, the president's house was officially named the White House by executive order. He also completely remodeled the building, doubling the family living space and adding a new wing (the "West Wing," although the term would not come into common usage until the 1930s) for the president and his staff. In 1909, President Taft, with the help of architect Nathan C. Wyeth, enlarged the West Wing, adding the first Oval Office.

The final major renovation of the White House took place under President Harry Truman when it was discovered in 1948, after the construction of the balcony on the south portico that bears his name, that the entire building was in danger of collapse. The brick that Hobson had used to line the stone façade was being stressed to its limits. Truman was forced to move across Pennsylvania Avenue into Blair House until 1952 while the interior of the White House was gutted and rebuilt.

RELIGIOUS OBSERVANCES
IN THE WHITE HOUSE

The White House is perhaps the most recognizable Washington, D.C., landmark, but it also plays seasonal host for many religious observances.

As you approach the White House on Pennsylvania Avenue, look just ahead to the left. In front of the White House and adjacent to the National Mall is the Ellipse, the site of the National Christmas Tree and the National Hanukkah Menorah. Despite a number of legal challenges, the Pageant of Peace takes place each year on the Ellipse. In addition to the National Christmas Tree and Hanukkah Menorah, it features Christmas trees from each of the states, a nativity scene, and nightly musical performances.

The tradition of placing a decorated Christmas tree in the White House began in 1889. While it started as a gathering for President Harrison's family and friends, the lighting of the White House Christmas tree has become a national tradition. In 1929, First Lady Lou Henry Hoover started the unbroken custom of first ladies trimming the "official" White House Christmas tree. In 1961 First Lady Jacqueline Kennedy began the tradition of selecting a theme for decorations, modeling it after Peter Tchaikovsky's *Nutcracker Suite* ballet. First Lady Laura Bush selected themes such as "Home for the Holidays" and "All Creatures Great and Small" to adorn the tree.

White House Christmas Tree (Courtesy of the White House)

Since 1878, American presidents and their families have celebrated Easter Monday by hosting an "egg roll" party on the White Houses lawn, one of the oldest events in White House history. The original site for this tradition was the grounds of the U.S. Capitol until Congress passed a legislation forbidding it. In response, President Rutherford B. Hayes officially opened the south lawn of the White House to local children and families to continue the tradition of egg rolling on Easter. Successive presidents have sustained this custom, canceling it only for occasional poor weather and two world wars.

Through the years, the White House has also been the site of prayer services and other religiously themed gatherings. After the Civil War, First Lady Lucy Hayes and President Rutherford B. Hayes hosted prayer services and hymn singing for members of the Cabinet, the Congress, and their families. They also renewed their vows before a Methodist minister in the Executive Mansion on their twenty-fifth wedding anniversary. President William McKinley also hosted gatherings in the Blue

I Pray Heaven To Bestow
THE BEST OF BLESSINGS ON
This House
And All that shall hereafter Inhabit it
May none but Honest and Wise Men overrule
under This Roof.

From a Letter of JOHN ADAMS

November MDCCC

Courtesy of the White House Historical Association (White House Collection)

President John Adams' Mantel, the White House

Room of the Executive Mansion on Sunday evenings in which he and visiting clergy would lead the group in hymn singing.

If you get the chance to go on the White House tour, be sure to visit the State Dining Room. The fireplace mantel contains a prayer by President John Adams:

> I pray to heaven to bestow the best of blessings on this house and all that hereafter inhabit it. May none but the honest and wise men ever rule under this roof.

Adams wrote these words to his wife, Abigail, after first moving into the residence in November 1800. President Franklin Roosevelt subsequently discovered Adams' words in the later years of World War II and had them carved into the stone fireplace below a portrait of Abraham Lincoln.

In 1953, President Dwight David Eisenhower hosted the National Prayer Breakfast out of a desire to meet with the House and Senate prayer groups and unite the nation's leaders under the common bond of faith. Over the years, the annual tradition has grown to include, by personal invitation, friends from all the fifty states and over one hundred countries throughout the world.

FAITH IN A PROVIDENT GOD

The World War II Memorial

*"The real fire within the builders of
America was faith—faith in a Provident
God whose hand supported and guided
them: faith in themselves as the children
of God . . . faith in their country and its
principles that proclaimed man's right
to freedom and justice."*

DWIGHT D. EISENHOWER
Thirty-fourth President of the United States

Chapter 12

THE WORLD WAR II MEMORIAL

World War II Memorial

With its open-air architecture and refreshing pool and fountain in its center, the World War II Memorial is one of Washington, D.C.'s most popular attractions. Fifty-six pillars and two forty-three-foot arches surround the main memorial plaza. The pillars are each inscribed with the name of one of the then forty-eight states in the Union, or one of the territories or commonwealths that sacrificed blood and treasure for the war effort. The Freedom Wall on the west side of the memorial is emblazoned with 4,048 gold stars, one for every approximately 100 deaths America suffered in the war.

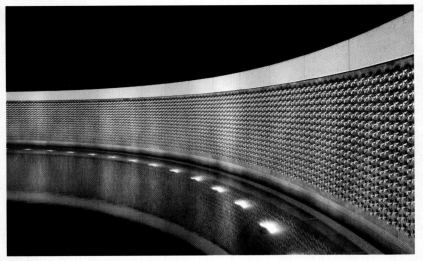

Freedom Wall, World War II Memorial

Two themes pervade the design and message behind the World War II Memorial: sacrifice and unity. It is the first national memorial commemorating both the sixteen million Americans who served in the Armed Forces during World War II (including the more than 400,000 who died) and the millions more at home who sacrificed to support the war effort. The memorial is a testament to the power of a free people, who, when faced with a threat to their country and the world, united to defeat tyranny.

Having officially opened on the sixty-year anniversary of D-Day, the World War II Memorial is one of the newest monuments in Washington, D.C., and, not surprisingly, is the most secular.

However, Eisenhower understood that our nation's rights and freedoms rested upon our firm faith in God. He said after the war:

> The real fire within the builders of America was faith—faith in a Provident God whose hand supported and guided them: faith in themselves as the children of God . . . faith in their country and its principles that proclaimed man's right to freedom and justice.

It is therefore unsurprising that Eisenhower and other American leaders talked often of this war as a crusade against evil. As Eisenhower himself said to the soldiers who were about to storm the beaches of Normandy on D-Day:

> You are about to embark upon the Great Crusade, toward which we have striven these many months. The eyes of the world are upon you. The hopes and prayers of liberty-loving people everywhere march with you.

This same passage can also be found on the Atlantic side of the monument.

During World War II, the government issued seventeen million Bibles to the soldiers with a message in them from Generals Eisenhower and Marshall. In addition, many of the government-printed World War II posters contained religious imagery. "This Is the Enemy" won a graphics award in 1943 and shows an arm with a Nazi insignia plunging a dagger through the Holy Bible. Another shows a German plane and Nazi soldiers attacking a crucifix. Eisenhower's address to the D-Day troops concluded: "Good Luck! And let us all beseech the blessing of Almighty God upon this great and noble undertaking."

A BRIEF HISTORY OF THE WORLD WAR II MEMORIAL

Ohio representative Marcy Kaptur first introduced legislation authorizing the construction of a memorial honoring World War II veterans on December 10, 1987. However, she had to introduce the bill three more times before it finally became law. On May 25, 1993, President Clinton signed Public Law 103–32, authorizing the American Battle Monuments Commission to select a site for a World War II Memorial in "Washington, DC or its environs." Congress and the president provided more specificity on the memorial's eventual location in October 1994 with Joint Resolution 227, which mandated that the memorial be located on the National Mall near the other monuments and memorials. Finally, on October 5, 1995, the American Battle Monuments Commission (with representatives from the National Park Service, the Commission of Fine Arts, the National Capital Planning Commission, and the newly formed Memorial Advisory Board) announced the memorial's final location. They chose the site of the Rainbow Pool, found on Seventeenth Street at the east end of the famous Reflecting Pool that sits between the Lincoln Memorial and the Washington Monument.

Once the location was finally selected, it was time to design the memorial. An open national competition was held, and in the summer of 1998 the Commission of Fine Arts and National Capital Planning Commission selected an initial design submitted by Friedrich St. Florian. The design, including the types of granite and marble to be used, was approved three years later and construction finally began in September 2001.

The fundraising campaign was led by former senator and World War II veteran Bob Dole, along with FedEx Corporation president and CEO and Marine Corps veteran Frederick W. Smith. Their efforts led to the raising of over $180 million dollars in private donations. Another $16 million was provided by the federal government.

The World War II Memorial was officially dedicated on May 31, 2004, Memorial Day. In his proclamation for a day of prayer for permanent peace, President George W. Bush offered these words on behalf of a grateful nation:

> Today, all who wear the uniform of the United States are serving at a crucial hour in history, and each has answered a great call to serve our Nation on the front lines of freedom. As we continue to fight terrorism and promote peace and freedom, let us pray for the safety and strength of our troops, for God's blessing on them and their families, and for those who have lost loved ones.

GOD'S WORK
MUST TRULY
BE OUR OWN

Arlington National Cemetery

*"The rights of man come not
from the generosity of the state
but from the hand of God."*

JOHN F. KENNEDY
Thirty-fifth President of the United States

Chapter 13

ARLINGTON NATIONAL CEMETERY

JAMES
CLANCY
WELLS
CAPT
637 TD BN
WORLD WAR I & II
KOREA
MEXICAN BORDER
APR 10 1897
SEP 1 1970

Cemetery Headstone, Arlington National Cemetery

Arlington National Cemetery offers a breathtaking view of nature, architecture, and our country's religious heritage. There are literally hundreds upon hundreds of memorials and graves decorated with religious imagery.

If you have a chance to absorb the breathtaking and awe-inspiring scenery of Arlington National Cemetery, take time to reflect on the bravery of those who lost their lives in service to our country.

A BRIEF HISTORY OF ARLINGTON NATIONAL CEMETERY

Old Guard Soldier, Arlington National Cemetery

Located just across the Potomac River in Arlington, Virginia, Arlington National Cemetery is the final resting place of over 250,000 of America's veterans and their families. But this bucolic 620 acres of green grass and elegant tombstones owned by the U.S. Army would shock anyone who saw the cemetery's humble beginnings.

During the Civil War, the location was an unkempt field of dilapidated graves marking mostly unidentified soldiers. Thomas L. Sherlock, the cemetery's historian said:

You would not have wanted to have a loved one buried there. It had none of the esteem or prestige it has today. We were burying two types of folks—soldiers who were unknown or soldiers whose families didn't have the money to return them to Pennsylvania or to North Carolina or to Ohio.

Back then, the land—along with most of Arlington County—was owned by Confederate general Robert E. Lee. Lee came into possession of the land through his wife, Mary Custis. Mary's father was the adopted son of another famous Virginian—George Washington.

After declining an offer to lead the Union Army, Robert E. Lee and his family moved from their property on April 22, 1861. Union forces quickly moved in and the federal government officially seized the land in 1862 after Mary failed to appear in person to pay $92.07 in taxes (although she had attempted to pay through an intermediary).

The Lee family tried to reclaim the land twenty years later. They won a decision in the Supreme Court, which held that the government had seized the land without due process. However, instead of forcing the government to move all the buried soldiers, General Lee's son accepted a $150,000 payment from the government for the property.

Secretary of War Edwin M. Stanton designated 200 acres of the land to be used as a military cemetery on June 15, 1864. Private William Christman of the 67th Infantry was the first soldier buried at Arlington, followed by thousands more Union soldiers during the war. However, few Confederate troops killed during the war are buried at Arlington. The majority of the approximately five hundred Confederate troops laid to rest at the cemetery all died after the war.

THE TOMB OF THE UNKNOWNS

One of the most popular sites in the cemetery, the Tomb of the Unknowns (also known as the Tomb of the Unknown Soldier) stands atop a hill overlooking Washington, D.C. The tomb holds the remains of unidentified American soldiers. The white marble sarcophagus sits over the remains of the grave of the unknown from World War I. The graves of the unknowns from World War II, Korea, and Vietnam lie to the west, marked by white marble slabs flush with the plaza.

In 1998 DNA tests showed the body of the unknown soldier from Vietnam to be that of Air Force First Lieutenant Michael Joseph Blassie. When his remains were moved, it was decided that the crypt set aside for Vietnam unknown soldiers would remain vacant.

Tomb of the Unknowns, Arlington National Cemetery

The inscription on the Tomb of the Unknowns reads, "Here Rests In Honored Glory An American Soldier Known But To God."

THE WOMEN IN MILITARY SERVICE FOR AMERICA MEMORIAL

The Women in Military Service for America Memorial is found at the Ceremonial Entrance to Arlington National Cemetery. Finished in 1997, it is the only major national memorial that honors women who have served in all branches of the military.

In 2006, the memorial hosted an exhibit celebrating the twenty-fifth anniversary of women in the Chaplain Corps titled "Wearing the Cross and the Tablets." The following quote from Charlotte Hunter, Lieutenant Chaplain, U.S. Navy, who served in Desert Storm, was displayed in the exhibit:

The ministry of all the chaplains was successful because we shared the experience of the people we served. We endured the same hardships, the same loneliness and longing to go home, the same fears about war.

America's success is also due to a shared experience: our faith in God as the source for our rights and blessings.

PRESIDENT JOHN F. KENNEDY'S MEMORIAL AND TOMB

One of the most famous gravesites in Arlington National Cemetery, marked by an eternal flame, is that of President John F. Kennedy's memorial and tomb. Inscribed upon it is his famous 1961 inaugural

Eternal flame over the grave of President John F. Kennedy, Arlington National Cemetery

address, in which he declared, "Ask not what your country can do for you; ask what you can do for your country."

Kennedy's inaugural address concluded:

With a good conscience our only sure reward, with history the final judge of our deeds, let us go forth to lead the land we love, asking His blessing and His help but knowing that here on earth, God's work must truly be our own.

Conclusion

LAUS DEO

It is poignant that the first rays of sun that illuminate our nation's capital each morning first fall upon the eastern side of its tallest building—the 555-foot monument to the father of our country. And there on its top, inscribed on the eastern side of the four-sided aluminum capstone are the Latin words *Laus Deo* ("Praise be to God").

These simple words, placed where they are for the eyes of heaven alone, are a fitting reflection of George Washington's deep conviction that the securing and maintaining of American liberty is owed to divine blessing, for which all Americans should humbly give thanks.

This book, *Rediscovering God in America,* is written from an historical perspective. Its purpose is neither theological, nor an effort to proselytize on behalf of any religious worldview. All Americans—both those who believe in God and those who do not share this belief—are equal in rights and duties under our Constitution and equal in deserving the respect of their fellow citizens.

Instead, the purpose of this book is to rediscover the historic source of American liberty and to rediscover the founding generation's understanding of what is required to sustain liberty in a free society. And to do this is to truly discover anew the centrality of God in American history and in the ongoing story of American liberty.

This rediscovery is presented herein in the form of a walking tour of our nation's capital where a free people preserve numerous references to God and religious faith by many of our most respected national leaders. Whether on parchment, inscribed in stone, metal, or concrete, or commissioned by artists and expressed in sculpture, reliefs, or canvas, these historic references are preserved for the sake of future generations.

As we have seen throughout this simple tour, the belief that our Creator is the source of American liberty is literally written into the rock, mortar, and marble of American history.

As we reflect on what we have learned on this walking tour of Washington, D.C., and of the Founding Fathers' vision for America, we should be mindful that a media-academic-legal elite is energetically determined to impose another, quite different and radically secularist vision against the wishes of the overwhelming majority of Americans.

This outlook rejects the wisdom of the founding generation as outdated and treats the notion that our liberties come from God as a curious artifact from the 1770s but of little practical importance for more enlightened times.

This elite is especially hard at work in the courts and in the classrooms where it is attempting to overturn two centuries of American self-understanding of religious freedom and political liberty.

In the courts, we see a systematic effort by this elite to purge all religious expression from American public life. The ongoing attempt to remove the words "under God" from the Pledge of Allegiance is only the most well known of these mounting efforts. These efforts are completely at odds with the views of the overwhelming majority of Americans.

Nevertheless, they have been successful to date because for the last fifty years the Supreme Court has become a permanent constitutional convention in which the whims of five appointed lawyers have rewritten the meaning of the Constitution. Under this new, all-powerful model of the Court, and by extension the repeatedly overturned Ninth Circuit Court, the Constitution and the law can be redefined by federal judges with few meaningful checks and balances by the other two branches of government.

Once five justices decided we could not pray in schools or at graduation or could not display the Ten Commandments, we lost those rights. If five justices decide we cannot say that our nation is "under God," then we will also lose that right. If they decide, for example, that the Constitution protects virtual child pornography on the Internet while having already ruled that the Constitution does not protect prayer and political speech, then they are not only arbitrarily rewriting the law of the land but are usurping the legitimate rights of the legislative branch of our government to make the laws.

This power grab by the Court is a modern phenomenon and a dramatic break in American history.

The danger is that the courts will move us from a self-understanding that we are one nation "under God" (where we have been endowed by our Creator with the unalienable rights of life, liberty, and the pursuit of happiness) to a nation all too familiar in history, a nation under the rule of the state where rights are accorded to individuals not by our Creator, but by those in power ruling over them. History is replete with examples of this failed model of might-makes-right—Nazism, fascism, communism—and their disastrous consequences.

In the classrooms, the very concept of America is under assault. The traditional notion of our country as a union of one people, the American people, has been assaulted by multiculturalism, situational ethics, and a values-neutral model in which Western values and American history are ignored, minimized, or ridiculed. Unless we act to reverse this trend, our next generation will grow up with no understanding of core American values. This will destroy America as we know it, as surely as if a foreign conqueror had overwhelmed us.

It is absolutely necessary to establish a firm foundation of patriotic education upon which further knowledge can be built; otherwise, Americans will lack understanding of American values and how important and great it is to be American. Thomas Jefferson wrote that the chief value of studying the past is "rendering the people the safe, as they are the ultimate, guardians of their own liberty . . . [H]istory by apprising them of the past will enable them to [be a] judge of the future."

It is important to understand what makes America so unique and why generations upon generations of diverse peoples immigrated to this great land for freedom and opportunity. If Americans do not appreciate America, and that for which she stands, then how can Americans be ready and willing to defend her? As Jefferson noted, Americans need to know where this country came from in order to know where it should go.

We should ensure that every student's understanding and appreciation of America is enriched by learning about the significant meaning of the founding documents, beginning with the Declaration of Independence in which Jefferson wrote the original proposition that we are endowed by our Creator with unalienable rights. It was this single acknowledgement by the Founders that established the firm foundation upon which our Republic was created and has endured for more than two and a quarter centuries.

Self-government is not easy. It is the most challenging and complex way in which human beings organize themselves. We, therefore, must make it a national priority to study American history—to learn the lessons of our successes and failures, and to learn why the conviction that our rights come from God is the surest foundation of our liberty and freedom.

Every president, member of congress, and federal judge has sworn to protect and defend the Constitution of the United States. Every citizen should bear this same responsibility. Yet, if we are to protect our Constitution and survive as a free people in an increasingly dangerous world, we must rediscover that each and every one of us is endowed by our Creator with certain unalienable rights that no government and no person can take away from us. We must also rediscover that inherent among these God-given liberties—especially in the public square—is the freedom of religious expression. We will never lose our liberty as a nation as long as we are free as a people to express publicly our belief in God.

In a letter written after the signing of the Declaration of Independence, Virginian John Page posed a rhetorical question to Thomas Jefferson: "We know the race is not to the swift nor the battle to the strong. Do you not think an angel rides in the whirlwind and directs this storm?"

We know from so many of his writings that George Washington was convinced that God was indeed an active agent in American history. In an especially poignant letter, Washington expressed this conviction to the Hebrew Congregation of Savannah:

May the same wonder-working Deity, who long since delivered the Hebrews from their Egyptian oppressors, [and] whose providential agency has lately been conspicuous, in establishing these United States . . . make the inhabitants, of every denomination, participate in . . . the blessings of that people whose God is Jehovah.

In his second inaugural address, Abraham Lincoln meditated that the Almighty had his own purposes in the Civil War, whose judgments Lincoln affirmed were still "true and righteous altogether."

Today, for many Americans, the angel still rides in the whirlwind and directs the fortunes of the great American political experiment in human freedom. And if we insist on courts that follow the facts of American history in interpreting the Constitution, as well as follow the firm conviction of the overwhelming majority of Americans, we will reestablish the right of every American to publicly acknowledge our Creator as the source of our rights, our well being, and our wisdom. And if we insist on patriotic education both for our children and for new immigrants, we will preserve the "mystic chords of memory" that have made America the most exceptional nation in history.

For a map of our walking tour and additional information please refer to the following website:
http://www.gingrichproductions.com/map